PRAISE FOR **I HAD A GOOD TEACHER**

"What a wonderful book—direct and deep, real and rich, filled with down-to-earth wisdom." —**Roshi Joan Halifax**, Abbot, Upaya Zen Center, and author of *In a Moment, in a Breath*

"Zen for the rest of us. A fine sampler of the kind of down-to-earth teaching for which Les Kaye has been so beloved by his students." —**Carl Bielefeldt**, Evans-Wentz Professor Emeritus of Oriental Philosophies, Religions, and Ethics, Stanford University, and author of *Dōgen's Manuals of Zen Meditation*

"In this lovely plainspoken book, Les offers the spirit of Suzuki Roshi Zen. Sometimes enigmatic, sometimes sweet, sometimes with stories of the past, sometimes timeless wisdom, all passed on to you with a kind heart." —**Jack Kornfield**, author of *A Path with Heart: A Guide Through the Perils and Promises of Spiritual Life*

"*I Had a Good Teacher* is such a marvelous collection of Les Kaye's talks and writings. Les was the first person Shunryu Suzuki ordained as a priest that didn't come from the San Francisco Zen Center. In these pages I can feel his authenticity and deep understanding. He's a perfect example of Suzuki's ideal of neither priest nor lay. Those who study with Les—in person or in this book—have a good teacher." —**David Chadwick**, author of *Crooked Cucumber: The Life and Zen Teachings of Shunryu Suzuki* and *Tassajara Stories*

"Each short, accessible chapter will help you experience, through words, a way of seeing and being that can't be reduced to words. Highly recommended." —**Brian D. McLaren**, author of *Life After Doom*

"Les Kaye is a pioneer in living a full Zen life in an ordinary life of work, family, and community. In *I Had a Good Teacher*, he brings alive the simplicity, ordinariness, and profundity of Zen practice. With fresh, engaging teaching, the book gives us a glimpse into Les's mature spirituality as a 'good student' of his teacher." —**Gil Fronsdal**, founding teacher, Insight Meditation Center, Redwood City, California, and author of *Everything Is Practice*

ALSO BY
LES KAYE

Joyously Through the Days: Living the Journey of Spiritual Practice

A Sense of Something Greater: Zen and the Search for Balance in Silicon Valley
with Teresa Bouza

Zen at Work: A Zen Teacher's 50-Year Journey in Corporate America

I HAD A GOOD TEACHER

PRACTICING
SUZUKI ROSHI'S
WAY OF ZEN

LES KAYE

MONKFISH
BOOK PUBLISHING COMPANY
RHINEBECK, NEW YORK

I Had a Good Teacher: Practicing Suzuki Roshi's Way of Zen Copyright © 2025 by Les Kaye

All rights reserved. No part of this book may be used or reproduced in any manner without the consent of the publisher except for in critical articles or reviews. Contact the publisher for information.

Paperback ISBN 9781958972809
eBook ISBN 9781958972816

Library of Congress Cataloging-in-Publication Data

Names: Kaye, Les, author.
Title: I had a good teacher : practicing Suzuki Roshi's way of Zen / Les
   Kaye.
Description: Rhinebeck, New York : Monkfish Book Publishing Company, [2025]
Identifiers: LCCN 2025011817 (print) | LCCN 2025011818 (ebook) | ISBN
   9781958972809 (paperback) | ISBN 9781958972816 (ebook)
Subjects: LCSH: Zen Buddhism. | Suzuki, Shunryū, 1904-1971. |
   Meditation--Buddhism. | Spiritual life--Zen Buddhism.
Classification: LCC BQ9265.4 .K394 2025 (print) | LCC BQ9265.4 (ebook) |
   DDC 294.3/927--dc23/eng/20250326
LC record available at https://lccn.loc.gov/2025011817
LC ebook record available at https://lccn.loc.gov/2025011818

Cover photo courtesy of Kannon Do
Book and cover design by Colin Rolfe

Monkfish Book Publishing Company
22 East Market Street, Suite 304
Rhinebeck, New York 12572
(845) 876-4861
monkfishpublishing.com

CONTENTS

Foreword by Norman Fischer vii

Editor's Introduction by Giuseppe M. Prisco xi

PART ONE
DHARMA TALKS

1. You Have to Get Wet 3
2. Building Monuments 7
3. The Honeybee Is Not Concerned with Failure 12
4. Preciousness 17
5. The Meaning of Activity 21
6. Monastic Practice in Everyday Life 26
7. We Are More Than Our Skills 30
8. Everyday Mind Is Always Finding Something Good . . . 35
9. Clearing Away Mind Ashes 39
10. Beyond Inspiration 42
11. The Pursuit of Happiness 47
12. Walking Past the Candy Store 52
13. Exploring the Territory 55
14. Life Is Perfect 60
15. Affirmation 64
16. The Soup of Our Life 67
17. Finding Your Rhythm 71

18. Love Without Attachment 74
19. The Natural World 78
20. The Alien and the Banana 82
21. Beauty Beyond Beauty 86

PART TWO
PERSONAL STORIES

22. The Magical World of Fish 93
23. Being Nice 96
24. The Bodhisattva Way 99
25. Hijacking Awareness 102
26. Liking Myself 105
27. Simplicity and Ease 108
28. I Had a Good Teacher 111
29. The Zen Practice of Steve Jobs 114
30. No Drama 118
31. Aim for the Heart 122

PART THREE
CLOSING WORDS

32. Questions and Responses 127
33. Bring Your Caring Nature to Life 139

Zen Ancestors Cited in This Book 143
Notes 145
About the Author 149
Kannon Do Zen Meditation Center 151

FOREWORD

I FIRST GOT to know Keido Les Kaye many years ago on a pilgrimage to Japan. A decade or so older than me, Les was among the first American Soto Zen priests to receive *Shiho*, or Dharma Transmission, and the purpose of our trip was for Les and two other priests who had received Shiho in our lineage, my teacher Sojun Mel Weitsman, and Tenshin Reb Anderson, to go up to the Headquarters monasteries of the School, Eiheiji and Sokoji, to do the required ceremonies for full certification as priests. It was a very exciting trip, full of all sorts of arcane Zen ritual and the details of Japanese Zen life. We met many Japanese Zen priests. We learned a tremendous amount about our tradition. And we hung out a lot together, and bonded.

Since then, over the years, I have met Les many times and practiced with him in many ways. I have known him to be unfailingly modest, flexible in his point of view, always practical, and in his understated way, very wise. He thinks about others and their needs and feelings; he doesn't push; he is generous and unflappable. This doesn't sound much like the enigmatic Zen Master of popular imagination. Les is perhaps the opposite: straightforwardly who he is, with no interest in being otherwise.

Maybe this is because from the start he was an engineer

with a steady job in a large corporation, often managing the work of others, and he was a family man. He did not live for years as a full-time resident monk at a Zen Center, as I and so many other of the early American Zen teachers did. Because of this, his practice always had to make sense in an ordinary life of rubbing shoulders with ordinary people. So he was always translating, asking about every aspect of Zen practice and teaching, "What can this really mean, how can this really work, in the everyday world that I, and so many others, inhabit?" If Zen practice is going to survive in and be of benefit to people in contemporary America, he reasoned, it had to work for him, in his situation, and for the many others whose lives were like his. So, from the start, this has been Les' approach. It comes, I believe, not only from his circumstances, but also from his character. It makes his way of practice especially valuable for our moment.

As Giuseppe mentions in his introduction, and as Les himself emphasizes in many places in these talks, trust is the magic of Zen practice. For some reason, unknown probably to himself, Les, from the start, trusted the practice and trusted his teacher, Suzuki Roshi. Les tells the story of attending, at the urging of a friend, one of Suzuki Roshi's early talks, and finding it a little odd and incomprehensible. But then he somehow found himself attending the next talk and the one after that, until very quickly he became one of the regulars, and the person who opened and closed the zendo and took care of things.

To trust our teacher is to trust ourselves, which is to trust the world and the truth of the world, which in Zen we call the Dharma. Such trust doesn't mean accepting something outside ourselves as authority or standard, it means finding our own way beyond self-willfulness. This is not an easy thing to do; it requires a guide who is willing to help us selflessly, without agendas. Over many many years, Les has proven himself to be such a guide. He is one of the most trustworthy people I have ever met. Les says, "I Had a Good Teacher." Over many years of faithful, trusting practice, Les has become that good teacher.

If there's a job description for Zen teachers, it would probably include a phrase like "just living your life." And doing this in such a way that others are included and can benefit simply from your daily example. This is not something you can write in a book. Which is why there has been, over the centuries, so much doubt about the writing and reading of Zen books. And yet, Les has written a few books. (Strictly speaking, he did not write this one). Which raises the question, how can you write such a book, and what can a reader gain from it?

In this book Les is talking, not writing, in his down-to-earth way, about how he feels about Zen practice, what it means to him, and how he views it. I admire his simple concrete expression and his wonderful use of metaphor. Maybe you can't explain Zen practice, but you can, if you have the knack, compare it to things readers already know, to give them a powerful image of what the practice is like. Such images are precious throughout the history of Zen, and world religions. They are treasured teachings, and they are tools for practice.

Zen practice, Les says, is like the ocean. If you want to know what it really is, there's no other way than to plunge in. To practice equanimity and continuous practice, he says, be like a bee that goes from flower to flower (in Les' wife Mary's garden) steadily and without hesitation, whether the flower yields a lot or almost no sweet. To do something for a self-serving motive is to build a monument to yourself, Les says, a monument you will have to polish and dust, but that will in the end crumble, as all monuments do. I hope you will enjoy, as I do, these and many other of Les' apt metaphors.

Les was in Silicon Valley before it became Silicon Valley. While he was quietly working and practicing Zen every day for decades, the valley grew up around him, so that by now, many of his students, like Giuseppe Prisco, are international tech people, extremely brilliant and sophisticated in their view of society and the material and theoretical world. That such remarkable people can be met by Les and his clear and unadorned Zen understanding, and take to it so marvelously (they perhaps need it more than the rest of us!) is a testament not only to Les' patient and effective way, but also to the power of the Dharma, and the need for it in this complex world. This is something Les talks about again and again throughout this book.

I so much enjoyed reading these talks. In them I feel not only the beauty of the Dharma, and the solidness of the practice in Les' temple, but also the love in his words for the students listening to him, and their love for him in preserving and shaping those words for readers now and to come.

NORMAN FISCHER
MUIR BEACH, CALIFORNIA

EDITOR'S INTRODUCTION

AFTER A HALF-DAY Zen meditation retreat in the Tuscan countryside with seven Dharma friends, the idea arose among us to collect some of the talks of my teacher, Les Kaye, and present them as a book.

Les was born and raised in New York City and moved to California in his twenties to work for IBM. After hearing that Zen Master Shunryu Suzuki was leading meditations in nearby Los Altos and in San Francisco, he became a Zen student and developed a strong practice at the two Zen centers and in his daily life of work and raising a family. Eventually, he became the head of the Haiku Zendo, which later become Kannon Do, was ordained a Soto Zen Buddhist priest by Shunryu Suzuki, served as head monk at Tassajara Monastery, and was given Dharma Transmission by Suzuki Roshi's son, Hoitsu. All the while, Les continued working at IBM until he retired, leading a kind of "double life." Because of the breadth of his experience, his Dharma talks have always been grounded in "the real world."

Books on Zen are often the initiatives of students rather than their teachers. Suzuki Roshi gave a series of weekly talks in the 1960s at the Haiku Zendo, and his students transcribed and edited them into *Zen Mind, Beginner's Mind*, still one of the most widely read introductions to Buddhist practice. And even though the Zen tradition explicitly states that understanding the teachings does not come from reading or studying—even ancient scriptures—there are thousands of books on Zen practice. I often wondered why, and now I find myself adding another work to the canon, appreciating for the first time the impulse to share the teachings of a wise and beloved mentor.

After completing my post-doctoral studies in Italy, I moved to Silicon Valley in 2000, like so many tech-minded people from around the world, and I worked on robotics-assisted surgical systems for Intuitive. I loved the life of "work hard, play hard," but eventually I began to feel out of balance. So, on a sunny Saturday morning in March 2008, I received zazen instruction at Kannon Do Zen Meditation Center, and in the following years attended a three-month practice period at Tassajara Zen Monastery, was ordained a Zen priest, and in 2012 moved back to Italy with my family. I'd spent four years studying Zen with a great teacher, surrounded by a large and experienced Sangha-community, and in Italy I continue to follow the same meditation schedule and to practice the vows of my priest ordination. I spent five more years bringing robotics to patients in need of microsurgical treatment, and in 2020, I retired from business to dedicate my time to Zen practice.

My friends and I had been practicing meditation together for months, and during our half-day retreat, we alternated sitting, walking, and silent breaks, and had a meal together in silence. At the end of the retreat, we returned our cushions to our cars and swept the floor. A few folks left right away, and the rest of us stayed on talking. One woman said she was disappointed we'd ended without having a chance to share a little about the experience we'd just had and to ask questions about the practice. Prompted by her request, my friends and I decided to assemble the words of Les Kaye, my teacher, in a book.

Meeting Les and receiving his teachings has been life-changing for me. His half-century of formal Zen practice alongside his life as a family man with a steady job are keys to understanding what he offers. I sometimes jokingly call him a suburban Taoist sage. I have observed Les closely over time, and I have seen his openness to and respect for students and practically everyone, allowing us to get to know him and build trust together. In this way, he taught me how to know others and to trust myself.

Still, Les is an elusive figure, almost invisible in his humility. We picture Zen teachers as charismatic and outgoing, expressing themselves poetically and sometimes with a shout. Les, on the other hand, is not like that. He isn't a scholar of ancient texts. He didn't build a large following or cultivate a high profile. What sets him apart is his capacity for guiding people in Zen practice within the context of daily life and its obligations. In his book *Zen at Work,* Les describes in granular detail how Zen training can take place not only in a mountain monastery but also at work and within families.

The archetype "Zen master" can represent a parent figure or an idealized wisdom keeper. And so, there is the inevitable disappointment when a student's psychological projections are shaken by a human being whose realization does not make him flawless. I mention this, as idealization can be a pitfall on the spiritual path. It's important that we not imagine Les—or any authority—as larger than life, but to appreciate him as a teacher who, at times, can help us.

Some teachings are particularly dear to Les. One is equanimity. Another is non-egoism. And a third is the commitment to continuous practice. Suzuki Roshi said Zen practice is like walking in the mist. You hardly notice it, but after a while, you realize you're wet. I have witnessed the moistness of Les Kaye, the silent joy with which he appreciates every moment, including his own and his students' successes. My Dharma friends and I hope you enjoy and benefit from this book as much as we have enjoyed bringing it to you.

GIUSEPPE GYOKUDO PRISCO
TUSCANY, ITALY

PART ONE

DHARMA TALKS

1

YOU HAVE TO GET WET

IF SOMEONE ASKS you, "What is Zen?" you might want to share some teachings you've heard, or talk about the history of Buddhism, or tell them something about your practice. Or you can say, simply, "Zen cannot be explained."

Zen master Yaoshan Weiyan (745-828 CE)[1] was asked to give a lecture at his monastery. He walked to the large chair at the front of the hall where he would sit when giving Dharma talks, and then, without saying a word, he turned around and went straight to his room. Later, his attendant asked him, "Why didn't you speak?" and Yaoshan replied, "There's no need to say anything." Then he added, "If you want to study intellectually, you can go to a philosopher. I don't need to speak. I just practice with you." That statement conveys the spirit of thousands of Zen masters who have dedicated their lives to their students and the practice.

Answering "What is Zen?" is like answering "What is the ocean?" To understand the ocean, you have to submerge yourself. *You have to get wet.* You can dive into the first wave or bend your knees and let the wave wash over you, or if your timing is right, you can walk in without being knocked over. But it's only after immersing yourself and engaging with water that

4 Les Kaye

you know what it means to be wet. If you stand at the water's edge and dip your toe in, you won't know the ocean. In Zen, we listen with our whole body, with our hopes, and with an empty mind, without trying to comprehend what it is intellectually, and without making a big deal of what we are doing. The only way is immersion.

There are thousands of academic studies on Zen, so many we probably won't be able to read them all. Some are thoughtful, some profound, and some share stories from deep within the history of Buddhism. Studying these can be help us understand the mind, the feelings, and the world views of Buddhists and scholars over the centuries. Explanations and studies can open the door and give us a glimpse, but we can't understand the practice with just our intellect. As a subject of study, Zen can be something we can talk or write about. But ultimately we can't really talk about it. We can only experience it viscerally, in an intuitive, feeling way. We understand practice in our gut, not in our head.

Here is a koan from the *Blue Cliff Record*.[2] Koans are stories that can bring us to the limits of logic, intended to provoke a deeper understanding. The fourth patriarch of Chinese Zen, Daoxin (580-651 CE) had three attendants, Guishan, Yunju, and Go-on. Daoxin asked Guishan, "With mouth and lips closed, how would you say it?" Guishan replied, "*I would ask you to say it!*" Daoxin told him, "I could, but if I did, I'd have no successors."

The Fourth Patriarch's question means: How do you express truth in everyday actions? His disciple, Guishan, says he can respond only if he doesn't use his intellect. Daoxin replies that if Guishan were to speak, he (Master Daoxin) wouldn't have any successors, affirming his student's response by saying that he doesn't rely on intellect either. Zen practice, and life, have to be understood through *experience*—like going in the ocean. To understand Zen practice, and our life, we need confidence and dedication. When we're confused, which is a lot of the time, we have to work to unravel the confusion. We keep practicing; time is not a consideration. "Practice without end" is our attitude, and it's this kind of confidence that awakens insight.

Here is a story from medieval Japan. In the fourteenth or fifteenth century, a man who wanted to master sword fighting, *Kendo*, went to study with the most famous swordsman of the day. The student asked, "How long will it take for me to master your way?" and the teacher replied, "If you want to master Kendo in three years, it will take a century. But if you don't worry about anything, even that you might be killed by your teacher, you'll master it immediately." Immediacy is the way. We must be ready to enter the great unknown.[3]

When we understand the importance of practice to our life, we'll have strong determination and we'll remind ourselves, "I will sit in meditation without moving. I'll move only when the *doan* rings the bell." Our practice is not for comfort or convenience; it's to encourage determination. And we make the effort to extend this attitude to everything we do. Of course, our determination can get short-circuited by desires and thoughts. So, we have to keep coming back to our zafu (meditation cushion) and renew our determination.

When we receive a gift from a friend, we don't say, "Actually, I wanted something else." We accept the gift without judgment. If we realize we wanted something else, we have to let that feeling go, come back to the mind of zazen, which is empty of desires, so that we can express our appreciation. Our attitude is accepting, and we emphasize serving others, not just ourselves and what we want. This is the way of the bodhisattva, literally an "awakening being."

Imagine if someone unborn were to arrive and ask, "What

is life? What is your life?" You could give them a long answer about various aspects of living, but the being from another dimension wouldn't understand. The best you can offer is to help them come alive. You don't need to say anything. When we meet people like this, we can try to help them come alive. The best Zen teachers always taught this way. They don't explain; they simply invite you to practice. The invitation might even be given in silence.

Suzuki Roshi gave many lectures to explain the teachings of Zen. Doing so was necessary for us, we were all new to the practice. But his greatest gifts were offered nonverbally. His way wasn't dramatic like the old masters. He was very quiet. What impressed me most was his continuous practice. He created opportunities so others could join him, and then he let us find our own way, gently, without trying to control and without scolding us. He let us make mistakes, try again, and learn. When we see that we're holding back from life, we don't need our teacher to scold us. We simply renew our determination to enter the water and get wet.

2

BUILDING MONUMENTS

ZEN PRACTICE IS not fully understood in the West. It hasn't been here that long, and it takes a while to understand what the practice is. Some people think Zen is a mystical practice, that through the practice they'll have transcendent experiences that will give them insight into hidden worlds they find subtly attractive.

But our practice isn't about seeing into other worlds. In fact, there's nothing mysterious about it. After practicing for a while, you'll see that Zen is quite straightforward. It's about developing an uncluttered, unclouded mind, and an unbiased view of life, free from delusion. Suzuki Roshi called this "Beginner's Mind." We practice not to gain access to mystical worlds, but to express our true self.

As we sit quietly and allow our mind to become free, we develop discipline, generosity, and confidence just by keeping our awareness on the present moment, whether we're sitting in meditation or whatever we're doing. Through awareness and the discipline and confidence that grow over time, we can *feel* our practice—and our lives—expressing our true, universal nature, what Buddhists call "Buddha nature," which is something that everyone and everything share and express.

When we see from this perspective, we understand that the so-called mystical is the ordinary, and that there's no distinction between them. When we set aside our mental clutter, our biases and attachments, we can express ourselves authentically and become our vast, true self that contains and is itself contained in everything and everyone everywhere, and at the same time impersonal. This may sound like metaphysics, but it isn't intellectual or even an explanation. There is no explanation. Only your practice will clarify your true self.

When we feel confused about the meaning of our life, or what we're doing with our life, it means we're attached to a conditioned concept of our self, which is a fictional yet addictive idea we have about ourselves. The point of Buddhist practice is to go beyond some made-up idea of who we are. Until we can go beyond that, we're not free. When we're addicted to an idea about ourselves, we'll always be attached to things that seem attractive but are simply temporary expressions of our true nature. It's this attachment to misleading ideas we have about our life that is the cause of a lot of anxiety and confusion.

To express our true self, we have to study ourselves carefully in every circumstance. This means to pay attention and stay engaged, so we can set aside each misleading idea as we become aware of it. Then the activities of our life will express our true self and we'll feel calm and settled. This is the mind of equanimity and it benefits us, and others, enormously.

In one of our chants, we recite, "I vow to save all sentient beings." There are a huge number of sentient beings, so this is a big vow, and its meaning can only be found in the practice. We might rephrase it to say, "I will save everyone, without judgment." This is a promise we make to ourselves and others—to live authentically, without adding anything, without seeking anything, just to live in the most straightforward way we can.

We're naturally moved by others' suffering and want to help

however we can. And we may be successful at relieving some difficulties, and people may say, "Thank you, I'm so grateful." But we're mindful of ourselves, even in the very moment we feel empathy and compassion and are effective in our actions. Otherwise, our effort may include greed, trying for example, to fill our own need to be helpful. "Look at me. I'm a helpful person." To study the self is to pay close attention and notice when our efforts come from delusion or how they develop either pride or shame. When we are dedicated to meditation practice, we might believe that sitting on the cushion is itself enough, and treat it as if it were some kind of magic. We have to be actively engaged in studying ourselves in every moment, especially our tendency to fool ourselves.

Many years ago, I was doing volunteer work. At one point, while talking about it to some friends, I realized how prideful I was becoming, and I had to acknowledge, "That's in me too." When we discover these kinds of things about ourselves, we might feel ashamed or embarrassed, but such discoveries give us the opportunity to do something about it, to stop walking around in delusion. Through these dimly recognized feelings, we build monuments to ourself and create more problems.

Some people think they're closer to God than we are. "My religion is better than yours. You don't see things the way I do, so you're wrong, a heretic." This view is based on a narrow view of the world and a misunderstanding of the nature of things. It, too, comes from a mind that creates monuments to itself.

These kinds of monuments are a burden. When we create them, they may seem shiny and clean, and we admire these aspects of ourselves. But like all monuments, they tarnish over time and lose their brightness. Kannon Do recently received a gift of a new Buddha statue. Sangha members had a discussion about where to place it. One idea was to put it under the Bodhi tree, a cutting we planted from the tree in India where the Buddha had his great awakening. But others pointed out that birds sit in that tree, and the Buddha would be covered in droppings in no time. Birds don't care about monuments. They just land on a tree's branches and do what birds do. They don't bow down or offer incense, chirping: "Wait, this is a monument."

Sooner or later in life, we need to find a meaningful site to place our monument without it becoming too soiled by droppings. And we shouldn't be surprised that some people don't care about the monuments we've created. That can bring up feelings of anger or sadness, even as we acknowledge that our statue is not who we are. When we notice our reactions to someone who isn't complimenting our monument, something important is taking place. If we don't dismiss these difficult feelings but accept that they, too, are in us, we can say, "Oh, I see!" When we do that, even though it makes us uncomfortable, we will find ways to take care of our challenging feelings too.

The monuments people revere and respect the most are old ones, created a long time ago. Monuments are things of the past. They look like they'll be around forever, but you can't hold on to them. Statues look solid, like they'll be here for thousands of years, but they come and they go. It's okay to have monuments, but we have to understand, they're not who we really are.

We can be mindful of how we do things, how we create things, what we're creating, and what is the true meaning of our creations. And at the same time, we have to be mindful about the ways we try to hold on to the things we create as if we need them to support who we are. This continuous process of self-observation is the "study" Dogen meant when he wrote: "To study Buddhism is to study the self."[4]

A fundamental teaching of Buddhism is that everything in this world comes from emptiness, as flowers come from the garden or rain comes from the sky. Everything is emptiness. And, at the same time, everything is form. In the *Heart Sutra*, it says, "Form is emptiness, emptiness is form."[5] We chant this every day. What does it mean?

Only when we have the calm and stable mind of equanimity can we understand the meaning of "Form is emptiness, emptiness is form." No one can explain what cannot be explained, but when we have the mind of equanimity our life explains what cannot be explained. From the mind of equanimity, we can respond to suffering and to the difficulties we encounter in life without the clutter of our personal desires. This is how we can take care of things in the present moment, without conjuring ideas of creating a monument to ourself. Then, whether the birds fly over and leave their mark, or not, there's nothing to be tarnished and we can find our true creativity.

With equanimity, we can stop trying to build a monument to ourselves. Suzuki Roshi said that the Bodhisattva's way is like railroad track: "The railway track is always the same. If it were to become wider, or narrower, it would be disastrous. Wherever you go, the railway track is always the same."[6] Our sincerity itself is the railway track.

When we see our tendency to build monuments, and its effect on us and others, we may feel troubled. That is the moment we can realize, "This is delusional, I don't want to live this way anymore. I have to put an end to it." That is the vow to save all beings. This is the feeling of sincerity. When we notice that we're off-balance, having a troubled or confused feeling, we can discover the motivation to continue our practice without getting caught by the desire for monuments. Practice means don't create monuments, and at the same time, don't worry about polishing the monuments you've created.

THE HONEYBEE IS NOT CONCERNED WITH FAILURE

WHEN WE'RE THE first to enter the zendo, it's a little dark and it's empty. As our eyes begin to adjust, seeing the zafus and chairs along the wall is inspiring and touching. We can feel the perfection, simplicity, and freedom in the cushions arranged so neatly in this quiet space. The zendo reveals something beyond ourselves—a universal connection and a potential in us—and it feels good. These cushions are ready to accept everyone who comes; they make no distinctions. An old teacher in China called human beings "skin bags." It's true, we are nothing but skin bags. These cushions are ready to accept all the skin bags of the world, all the flavors, to sit quietly and to practice being, just being.

After the period of zazen ends, we straighten our space and leave the cushions ready to accept whoever comes next, like a perennial flower that blooms year after year. Eventually we come to regard each zafu as life itself. Today someone appears at this cushion, tomorrow someone else. The practice each day is the same and also not the same.

The life of the zendo and the life of the zafu are the same as our life. The zafu is more than a black cloth bag filled with kapok, because we bring *ourselves* to it. When we sit in meditation, we *are* the cushion and the cushion is us. When our minds are quiet and still, we touch the source of existence and express our infinitude. This is why the zendo is a holy place. Creative timelessness is expressed in the silent activity here, and it's here that our potential comes alive. With our upright posture and firm attitude, we pay respect to timelessness and to our vast potential.

In the Lotus Sutra, a renowned Mahayana Buddhist text, someone asks, "What if a young boy is teaching and the master says, 'I will serve whoever explains the Dharma.'"[7] The Dharma is about letting go of the self. What's important is not so much the words, but to experience the true meaning of *explain* and *serve*.

There are three ways one might experience explaining. The first is to listen to someone we think is knowledgeable who can explain a truth in a logical, intellectual way. This is how we usually expect to learn something.

In our practice, however we understand explaining differently. In Zen, we experience "explaining" through our practice. We practice all day long, and when we meditate, we take care of our posture, our cushion, the zendo, others, and ourselves. Thus, the second way to experience explaining is through your own mindful activity. No words are needed when we let our relationships with people and things explain the Dharma.

There is a third way to experience explaining, and that is to let our life serve life without waiting to hear or read what to do or what the truth is. When we do that, we let our life serve life, and we see that life itself is always explaining the Dharma.

Most people prefer the first way, to listen to a knowledgeable person's words. But I believe, more deeply, they really want the third kind. Everyone wants the freedom of selflessness.

For that to happen, we have to experience the second way

of explaining, through the practice. We have to know how to take care and be in service with our own life. Thus, we have to learn the meaning of *service*.

"I will serve those who explain the Dharma." So, we take care of that which explains the Dharma. Serving precedes explanation. The explanation is in the taking care. We practice giving, and we practice taking care of what takes care of us.

When we are in the zendo, we don't sit facing each other, we turn our face to the wall.[8] Although we turn our gaze toward the wall, facing the wall is facing the whole world, facing everything, ready for anything, and giving up everything. This kind of practice, facing the world, enables us to see the whole universe with our physical posture and the posture of our mind.

When we sit together in a zendo, our backs to each other, facing the world, we are the vast body facing the vast body. If you try to analyze this statement, it will seem confusing. It's not logical. Don't use your mind to try to understand. Let the explanation unfold with your practice. Only when you sit with an empty mind can the vast body face the vast body.

When we talk about an empty mind, or the emptiness of mind, it doesn't mean a blank slate. An empty mind is not a mind that doesn't think. An empty mind is the mind that knows how to think and when it needs to think. So, when we say "empty mind," we mean we are allowing our thinking mind to rest in zazen.

Zen is the practice of living in each moment completely. Most people believe it's impossible. "I have too many problems, too many responsibilities." Or, "It's too hard. My life is too complicated." Further, they may feel, "When I don't have any more problems, I'll be able to live fully." This is a misunderstanding because the problems we have are mostly ones that we ourselves generate. We create problems in our life when we don't know ourselves, when we don't know who we are. These

I Had a Good Teacher   15

problems are created by ego, by misunderstanding ourselves. Even when we know ourselves, we still create problems. But these are the kinds of problems that help us, because there is no ego involved. It's fine to have problems in life if you don't create them by not knowing who you are.

At my home, we have a garden with lots of flowers and plants. The bees come to the flowers for the nectar, and I like to watch them. Sometimes a bee will go from plant to plant and flower to flower. It may go to one and leave right away, and go to another and leave again, because it's not finding anything. Then it will land on a flower that does have nectar. The bee is always trying, often not connecting, but the honeybee does not recognize failure even when a plant she visits has no nectar. The honeybee has no concern for her scorecard, efficiency, or the productivity of her efforts. It visits many plants, and each visit brings life. Without any special effort or any idea of success, the bee is just doing her thing, which is ordinary and universal at the same time. She has no need to think about it. Each bee landing on and touching a plant is life itself. She brings life in each visit, without any concern for failure.

We can learn a lot by observing bees. Our world is incredibly fast and busy, and there's a great emphasis on efficiency and saving time. But the more we do, the less efficient we may be. Zazen practice is efficient in a universal sense, although it looks as if we're doing nothing. Usually, we measure efficiency by analyzing the results of our efforts. We count the number of objects we make in a certain period of time. We calculate how far we've traveled in a certain period of time. Efficiency is understood by analyzing the results, but if we want to understand our life, it won't come by that kind of analysis. They're just numbers, they're not us. We cannot understand our life or our self in terms of efficiency.

When you come to this practice, when you start to explore

or engage in your spiritual life, it may seem vague and ambiguous, and you don't know what it is. You can't measure it. There's no efficiency. So you wonder, "What is it? What does it mean? I'm drawn to it, but I don't understand it." Allow it to be vague. Let it be ambiguous. Allow it to be confusing and subjective. Don't try to sort out or clarify your spiritual activity through reason, and don't worry that it may seem to be inefficient, such as, "I meditated for forty minutes today, and I never had a moment of inner silence. It's seriously inefficient." This isn't something to worry about. Don't let it upset you. Let it be vague, inefficient, and ambiguous. Don't worry if you're productive or not productive. Just have confidence in the instinct and intuition that brought you to practice, and have confidence in yourself.

Our practice is about letting go of our attachment to literal thinking and being ready to receive explanations however they appear. We don't need to analyze our life to understand it. Through practice, we *will* understand. Through our practice we will understand ourselves, and this understanding that unfolds moment-by-moment through our activities is the greatest efficiency.

4

PRECIOUSNESS

M Y WIFE MARY was a landscape designer for more than thirty years, designing gardens for private homes and, once in a while, for businesses. Of course, that means we have a wonderful garden at home. On the border of our garden, next to a walkway, Mary planted peonies. That was about forty years ago, starting them with rhizomes from her mother's garden in Oklahoma. Rhizomes grow horizontally beneath the surface; they look like roots and don't send up a lot of flowers. Her mother did the same thing sixty years earlier, so our peonies were planted one hundred ago. And she said to me, "These are very precious to me."

When we talk about things of the world and say, "This is rare," "This is beautiful," "This is special," "This is out of the ordinary," we elevate these things to the category of precious. We attribute the quality of preciousness to material things that we feel are unique, rare, priceless—goods to be treasured and protected, and not to be squandered. We also attribute the quality of preciousness to intangible things like love, respect, support, and acceptance. When we don't feel these things, we miss them and realize how precious they are to us. And when we do feel we've been given respect, support, and love, it awakens in us feelings of confidence and optimism.

And of course our health is precious to us, especially when we realize how vulnerable we are. And on a larger scale, we all feel that life itself is precious. But do we understand why we feel that way? Are we clinging to life simply because we don't want to lose it? Or is there something else we can point to, the basis for the priceless nature of our life?

Our practice teaches us that life is more than our possessions. It's not limited to material things, or even good feelings or health. When our understanding of life goes beyond our possessions, tangible and intangible, we can see life's universal, spiritual nature. This is the practice to see beyond our possessions, that life itself is precious and sacred. Each life is the unfolding of something vast, though we can't say what it is, we can't describe what that feels like. Sometimes we call the vastness of our life Buddha, sometimes we call it God, sometimes our true nature, or the ground of being. Whatever name we give it is not important. It's just tentative. What's vital is the understanding of its nature.

We cannot escape birth and death, and at the same time, life is boundless. In its largest sense, life has no beginning, no end, no shape, and no limits. Still, we put limits on our life, and so it appears to us in the form of a game or even combat. When you look around and see what people are doing, you'll see that they regard life as a kind of project to work on, and the only question becomes, "Am I winning?" And as we age, we ask, "Did I win?" These questions reflect a misunderstanding of the true nature of our life. Even if we feel we're winning, that kind of winning can't help us appreciate life's preciousness. "How is it possible to win something that is limitless?"

The world has become complex and speedy. The pace of the modern world gives us little opportunity to recognize the truth of the life we have, because we're always under pressure to "win" or "add value." When we try to grasp the ungraspable, we only become confused. But when we don't trouble ourselves about scoring or defeating or obtaining a personal possession, we can begin to understand the meaning of *precious* and begin to understand what our life is truly all about.

It's never too late to arouse the mind of spirituality. This arousal begins with a subtle feeling that life's precious nature is rooted in the non-material and the non-emotional. The precious nature of our life is beyond what we can see or feel or touch. When we have that sense, we have a strong desire to see life as it really is, to fully embrace and trust it, even when the material and emotional things we cherish are taken from us. The starting point for the arousal of the mind of spirituality is a dim, emerging awareness that everything in life is sacred and precious.

Our true spiritual practice, more than the rituals we might perform, is reflected in the mindfulness and respect we bring to our daily activities and to our relationships. We do it by avoiding careless judgments, careless words, and insensitive actions. When we are careless or show disrespect for others or for what we do, it's like tossing trash into a clear, life-giving stream. But when we take responsibility for the consequences of our words and actions there is little chance we'll pollute the world because we recognize its precious nature.

Everything in our world is precious, not just my wife's flowers. That includes even the things we're not fond of. This understanding grows as we practice and learn to accept with grace whatever comes to us: the fights, difficulties, confusion, heartbreak, joy, and wisdom. When we understand that this acceptance is our work and our spiritual practice, we discover friendship and compassion for everything—without exception.

Without an open-hearted acceptance, our life becomes a

game or a project or even a war, and we become overwhelmed with grasping. This world we live in is actually all-inclusive; there are trees, friends, animals, stones, parents, oceans, strangers, and storms, and it's all precious. It's all sacred. But without the vision that arises from our spiritual practice, we forget the true nature of our world and we're left with a small view of things and of ourselves. To appreciate the inherently precious quality of our world, we have to develop a large, unlimited vision of the meaning of our life. This is our practice.

THE MEANING OF ACTIVITY

Buddhist teachings are remarkable, encouraging, shocking, and profound, and when you first come across them some seem absurd. "Why would they say that?" "I wonder what this means."

One of the key teachings says, in essence, "All beings are inherently enlightened." When you first hear that, you might think, "It doesn't feel like it." If everybody is inherently enlightened, why do we suffer? And why do we squander our inherent enlightenment and create even more suffering?

In one of his talks, Dogen, the founder of the Soto school of Zen Buddhism in the thirteenth century, pointed to a trap in Zen practice, which he called the desire for fame and gain. Here is a little bit of what he says:

> People nowadays rarely seek the truth. Deficient in practice and realization, they seek recognition for their effort and understanding. This is delusion on top of delusion. You should abandon such confused thinking. Among those who study the way it is rare to find determination for true dharma.... From the time of the Tathagata to this day there have been many who have been concerned with fame and

gain in the study of the way.... You should know that there is a disease for fame and gain among practitioners of the way.... Do not forget the aspiration that arises when you first seek the way. When you arouse the aspiration for enlightenment you do not seek dharma in order to be respected by others. You abandon fame and gain, and without veering off you aspire to attain the way.... But foolish people, even those with way-seeking mind, quickly forget their original aspiration and hope for offerings from humans and devas.... This is a hazard of practice.[9]

He calls the desire for fame and gain a disease. It is a hunger, a deep need like that of a child who wants a sugary drink or a candy that tastes sweet for the moment, but in the long run, can't satisfy us. We simply want more, and it's a kind of addiction. Dogen talked about fame and gain in terms of our practice, but what he says applies to all human activities.

In Buddhism, there are teachings about hungry ghosts who can only experience transient moments of excitement. They demand more and more but they can never be satisfied. Two of these hungers are for fame and for gain.

As Dogen points out, many practitioners don't recognize their attachments or their addictions, and in general people do recognize them but cannot stop. When we first come to the practice, it may be because we want understanding, enlightenment, wisdom. We want to be free from our hungry ghost tendencies. But we humans are foolish, and as he says, the mind can be stubborn and we may forget our original way-seeking mind and instead turn toward satisfying our hunger for sweets.

How do we overcome this tendency? We have to continuously renew our original spirit and practice without any idea of gaining something for ourselves. In no-gain practice, we have a chance of making our best effort. Continuous renewal means *continuous practice*, otherwise our karmic activity pulls us back without us realizing it. So, we have our practice, we have the zendo, and we have each other to encourage us to continue our zazen together.

Kannon Do and other Zen centers provide an opportunity to sit together regularly. And sitting together, we have a chance to recognize our karmic activity, the activity of a self-oriented mind. And when we're able to recognize this, we can make a conscious decision to let go of that desire and return to being fully alive in the present moment. Even if we don't recognize our karmic activity, if we sit with trust in our practice, these tendencies will diminish and even dissolve without our noticing. The letting go that we talk about in our practice will happen by itself. We can call this "Buddha's activity."

The attitude we must keep in our practice is to trust Buddha's activity and make it *our* activity. When we trust our zazen practice and put our best effort into it, we sit with Buddha. It doesn't mean asking Buddha for help. It means we trust that Buddha *is* continuously helping. Whether we know it or not, Buddha's activity is always at work through us.

A young man came to visit Suzuki Roshi in the early days of the San Francisco Zen Center, in the 1960s, and said, "I've recently come to this country, and I want to learn about Zen. Can you teach me?" Suzuki Roshi replied, "I sit every morning. You can join me."

Suzuki Roshi was inspiring for his selflessness, and he was the symbol and the meaning of practice. When he said, "I sit every morning and you can join me," he was really saying, "Let Buddha help you. Trust that your activity is Buddha's activity." This is the way to understand what our practice is.

If, after a time, we have the feeling that our practice isn't working, it means we have not yet learned to trust the practice. It's like asking, "Why isn't somebody helping me? I've been sitting and nothing happens, who's withholding the good stuff from me?" When we feel or complain that our practice isn't working, it means we don't appreciate that help is already here. When we make our best effort, when we make a sincere effort, when we continue our determination, we can appreciate that help is already here and there's no need to wait for help or to wait for enlightenment.

Dogen traveled from Japan to China to meet monks there, because Zen was new in Japan and his teacher had asked him to go to China to learn more about authentic Zen practice. After a difficult and dangerous voyage, Dogen stayed on the ship for a few days to get accustomed to being in such a new place. An elderly Chinese monk, then in his sixties, came aboard the ship to purchase some Japanese mushrooms. In the thirteenth century, that was old. Originally from Sichuan Province, he had been away from home for forty years. The old monk had visited monasteries in all corners of China and chose to study under Zen master Rujing on Tiantong Mountain, where he'd been appointed chief cook. He had just travelled twenty miles by land to purchase mushrooms from the Japanese ship.

Dogen was deeply impressed by the monk's devotion and invited him to stay on board the ship that night. He said that if he did so, it would disrupt the monastery schedule. Dogen asked him why someone else couldn't prepare the meals and why a monk with his seniority still had to work so hard, rather than just practicing sitting meditation. The old monk left abruptly, saying loudly, "My good man from a foreign land, you still do not understand *discipline*. You still don't know the meaning of words."

Dogen was startled and asked him to explain. The monk said, "Come to Wuang Mountain and study the meaning of the teachings." Then he stood up and left the ship before dusk.[10]

The cook's reply disturbed Dogen, who realized how

intellectual his own practice was in comparison. The cook's way opened a wholly new path for Dogen, marking a shift from searching for a final answer to the "Great Doubt" to a renewed aspiration for the attainment of the Way. Single-minded discipline, he realized, is necessary for practice. It's sometimes called "Right Effort," or, simply, "knowing how to work." We usually want results from the work we do—some tangible or verbal reward. We're hungry for recognition and appreciation. When we contemplate an activity, if we don't anticipate receiving a reward, we might not do it.

In our practice, we have a different view of effort. We call it "selfless." We don't care about rewards, fame, or gain. But, as Dogen observed, to keep our original, pure mind is unusual. The cook made an effort "for effort's sake," not for a reward. When we do that, it's Buddha who is doing the activity. In that moment, we are Buddha. The fame and gain that Dogen spoke of are for power, fame, or control. These are prevalent attitudes everywhere, not just in the worlds of politics and commerce. Fame and gain include pride, stubbornness, self-interest, carelessness, blaming, and being unforgiving—in other words, clinging to small mind.

It's painful to be a hungry ghost. We can feel the pain of a mind that's interested in fame and gain, and when we feel that pain, we will come to practice. With determination, we can move toward the selfless mind of the old cook. We can call this the "original pure mind" or "Beginner's Mind." When we practice, we return to our Beginner's Mind over and over. Then we will know how to make a right effort. Free of seeking fame and gain, we will stop squandering our inherent enlightenment.

6

MONASTIC PRACTICE IN EVERYDAY LIFE

For the past hundred years, American society has become overwhelmed by the rapid growth of technology and the increasing abundance of material goods. While providing significant advances in health, safety, and comfort, they have created an environment that conditions individuals to be concerned with what they can attain and possess. We as a society have been excited by consumer goods for the past two or three generations, increasingly oriented towards having the newest, best, biggest, and most entertaining next thing. We have been brainwashed into believing that "pursuing" and "possessing" are virtues.

When a culture becomes overwhelmed by materialism, its spiritual life diminishes. People become less concerned with who they are in a deep sense, what is helpful, and what is the best way to relate to others. Without viewing the world with our spiritual eyes our life becomes confused and our view superficial, so that we can no longer tell the difference between what is good and what just looks good. Without spiritual awareness, we're fooled by appearances and become slaves to preferences and fashions. We even mistakenly think, *If it looks good, it must be good.* To possess fashionable things may provide assurance that we're okay, but in their pursuit we short-circuit reflection and selflessness.

In recent years, many people have started to notice how fulfilling desires is not sufficient to provide meaning in their lives, and the empty feeling they have when they emphasize consuming. And so we are starting to ask, "What should be my orientation? What is the point of my life? How then shall I live?" With these spiritual questions, we start to seek real meaning. Spiritual practice starts with recognizing the thin nature of pleasure, how attachment robs us of understanding by distracting us from living an authentic life. We come to practice seeking what is real, *something* beyond ideas of truth and beauty, right and wrong. We want to know what that "something" is, to get to the heart of life.

People differ in their ideas of what spiritual practice is really about. Some are skeptical of the whole concept, and have objections like, "It will diminish my creativity and drive," "It will interfere with normal, everyday life," "It requires too much austerity." But these aren't valid concerns. Material and physical comforts are not inherently bad. Having fun, feeling satisfaction, and working with others on everyday problems are all okay. Yet we humans are easily overwhelmed by pleasures and possessions and the freedom to do whatever we like at any time without restriction.

Material things surround us. They stimulate our desires and attachments and can interfere with our understanding, and our relationships with each other, and especially with our peace of mind. Training at a monastery limits our choices, but after some difficulty, the mind learns to let go and accommodate the strict environment. This training helps us give up striving. We feel content with a few necessities. The taste of a freshly unearthed carrot becomes simply magnificent.

The most valuable part of monastic training is how it pushes the mind to see itself and the ways it struggles with attachments. This kind of training clarifies desires and delusions so they can be accepted, and then let go. Plus, following the monastic schedule teaches us how to work, in the deepest sense. So, practicing at a monastery or attending a Zen retreat can be quite valuable. But not everyone can take a break from their life to spend time in a monastery, so we have to learn how to practice in ordinary circumstances.

The vital ingredient for practice is not a special place; it is the deep desire to understand the truth of our life and of our world, beyond appearances and delusions. To truly practice, we have to have the courage to accept what we discover about our self, and to continue to practice in the everyday world. It takes determination to continue when practice becomes physically or emotionally challenging and the distractions of daily life offer an easy escape.

That being said, we can practice non-attachment anywhere, anytime, and we can watch our mind carefully so we don't become overwhelmed. The most important point is to face our tendencies, to let our everyday life be our monastery. Suzuki Roshi said, "I don't expect every one of you to be a great teacher, but we must have eyes to see what is good and what is not so good."

When people recognize the limitations of material possessions and comforts, they will seek balance in their lives and turn toward spiritual practice to understand who they are—intrinsically—and what life is like beyond appearances. A life limited to affluence, comfort, and excitement leaves nothing to fall back on when we ache to understand life's larger meaning.

Material success is not a true measure of the quality of a society or an individual. Our true measure is seen in our "softer," non-material relationships—how we support, care for, encourage, and acknowledge each other. To practice is to feel the presence of "something" greater than what we can see, think, hear, or feel. Even if we are rather good at these activities, we practice because we know that they just come and go, without permanence. And we want to know their sources and their meaning.

WE ARE MORE THAN OUR SKILLS

THE PURPOSE OF Buddhist practice is to learn how to live authentically in accord with our true self, continuously, moment after moment. Buddhist teachings encourage us to live in freedom from dependency on appearances, on what seems real, but is not.

In Zen practice, we don't emphasize attaining some special kind of mind. We don't emphasize any particular teaching or anything that could be called sacred, as there is nothing uniquely sacred and no state of mind exclusively special. Zen doesn't emphasize ideas or concepts, even those that are inspiring. Instead, we emphasize how to bring the truth of the teaching into everyday life, engaging ourselves completely in each present moment. We do that so we can be alive to whatever is unfolding, and whatever is unfolding in us. When we speak of Zen practice, or when we say *Zen*, we mean all the activities of life.

How can we bring an ancient tradition like this into the modern world? We don't really know yet. Today's world is profoundly different from the way things were when Buddhism began 2,600 years ago and as it has evolved. Until recently, almost all practitioners were monks living in monasteries.

They had no personal lives outside the monastery gates and travelling between monasteries. They had few personal possessions, and little time to do anything personal. They spent one hundred percent of their time and energy studying and practicing the teachings which had been handed down to them from the time of the Buddha.

Practitioners in those days had no concerns with family, politics, or economics. They focused only on practicing the Buddha's way. Today, in the twenty-first century, Zen practitioners are mostly lay people like you and me, and we have to weave our practice into a daily life that includes personal needs and responsibilities. There are relatively few monks in the modern world, it's lay people who want to stay lay people who are interested in the practice. They don't want to drop out and go to a monastery. They have to work, be with their families, and serve their communities.

How do we establish a practice in this environment, with its pressures, confusion, and forces beyond our control? That's the question of today's Zen students. Practitioners of old didn't worry about any of these things. They simply took care of their practice, and their temples and monasteries.

When newcomers arrive at our zendo, many have the impression that Zen is very formal. They see a well-kept space—carefully arranged cushions lined up uniformly, an altar with a statue of the Buddha, with incense burning and oil lamps lit. The zendo is a picture of order and discipline. And it's true, this is a formal practice. We have set routines and a space that is isolated from the busyness of everyday life, from ambition and concerns about success, and, at least for a specific period of time, from the tensions of everyday life.

In the zendo, we create community among like-minded people, sharing our spiritual practice and our lives. The energy of the practice can actually be felt in the zendo, because we are all here together, not casually or as separate individuals. The community is serious about finding and expressing our spiritual nature, and we do that rather formally. But at the same time, we emphasize the importance of personal relationships among Sangha members and with our visitors.

Part of our practice is to be attentive, caring, supportive, and flexible. So, while we practice in a formal way, we can also be informal and fun-loving. These are some of the qualities of Zen practice in the modern world. If you visit monasteries in Japan, they may not seem fun-loving. They are considerably more formal even than we are here, but Japan has a different cultural reality. No matter how we have to modify the forms of practice to fit the modern world, if we keep the original intention and attitude, the spirit and determination of the Buddha and his successors will continue with us. The forms and formalities are to remind us not to be separate from our true self. We are always with others who are also seeking freedom and truth.

But it's not easy to keep this original attitude. We vow to keep that intention, and then we notice it slipping away. Keeping the original attitude is not so easy, because we need to be a part of our society and part of our culture. This is the challenge: We don't want to drop out, so we have to be creative in establishing our authentic life in both the material and spiritual dimensions.

All beings need to develop skills in order to survive. From the smallest insects to the animals in the forest, from the fishes to ourselves, we need skills to survive and to live authentically. This has been true since the beginning of sentient life on Earth. But if we label ourselves by, for example our skill or occupation, we limit our role in life to using those skills. But our skills aren't who we are.

Using our skills, we can provide society what it wants.

Thanks to our skills, we can have a comfortable life. Our skills are necessary for us to survive and for society to thrive. But consider this: Does fulfilling your social role with your skills really fulfil you? What do you truly want and need?

Zen practice is a door to the wider world, a way to see and understand ourselves and our roles without boundaries, to see who we are beyond dependency on our personal skills. Machines have skills. Their features perform specific functions. But we're not machines. Focusing just on skills makes us mechanical. When we overemphasize skills, we forget who we are. In addition to our skills and intellect, we need heart and we need feelings. We need the parts of ourselves that care, connect with, and embrace life. This is the foundation of Buddhism and of all spiritual practice.

Our greatest skill is not mechanical and not functional. It is to see the workings of our own mind. To notice when we get off-balance and when we act without authenticity. When we see this in ourselves, we can return to balance. But if we become overly focused on our skills, our creativity, and our successes, we will have a narrow view of our life. This narrow view is called the "self" or the "Ego," and it blocks the view of our unlimited self.

In a chapter called "God Given" in *Zen Mind, Beginner's Mind*. Suzuki Roshi says, "When we repeat: 'I create, I create, I create,' soon we forget who is actually the 'I' which creates the various things.... This is the danger of human culture.... Because we do forget who is doing the creating, ...we become attached to material or exchange value."[11] *The danger of human culture* and being caught up in *the idea that I do the creation*, these are strong words.

When Suzuki Roshi says, "I create, I create," he means, "I'm using *my skills to create something*. When we think that way, we can become very proud of what we do, and we won't fully understand what we're doing or making, which leads to problems. And it's a narrow view of ourselves. We practice so we can have a wider view of ourselves and of our life, and see who we are, in total, without restriction. We practice so we can use our skills to improve our life and help others, always remembering we are more than our skills.

8

EVERYDAY MIND IS ALWAYS FINDING SOMETHING GOOD

DESHAN WAS A NINTH-CENTURY Chinese Zen master and a noted authority on the Diamond Sutra. As such, he was often engaged in intellectual activity. He lived and studied with his teacher Longtan for many years. One night as Deshan and Longtan were walking together down the dark corridor of the temple, Longtan suddenly blew out Deshan's candle and they were in utter darkness. At that moment Deshan's mind opened.

Su Dong Po was a layman, a poet famous for his spiritual attainment and understanding of Buddhism. One day on a journey in the mountains, he heard the sound of a stream in the valley below and his mind opened. He wrote this verse:

> The sound of the valley is his great tongue
> The colors of the mountains are his pure body
> In the night I have heard the 84,000 hymns
> But how to tell people the next day?

Dogen, who founded the Soto Zen school in Japan in the thirteenth century, commented: "It is a pity that from ancient times up to the present there are people who do not realize that the universe is proclaiming the actual body of Buddha. It is regrettable that many only appreciate the superficial aspects of sound or color."[12]

The eighth-century Chinese Zen master Xiangyan lived in a hermitage for a time. One day while sweeping leaves outside his hut, a stone flew from his broom into a bamboo stem. Hearing the sound, Xiangyan's mind opened.[13]

The literature of Zen is famous for dramatic stories like these of people who were dedicated to practice and had a big enlightenment experience. These stories have encouraged many people to practice, hoping to have a sudden experience themselves, awakening to understanding and putting an end to confusion. The idea of attaining a sudden experience and having a miraculous transformation may be tempting, but in my mind leads nowhere. The problem is that it focuses on the intellect that will gain new knowledge and thus become wiser. But this is relying on rational thinking, mental ideation. It's not the meaning of "mind opened."

If you've ever gone scuba diving or snorkeling in Hawaii or another exotic place, your attention is totally absorbed by the dramatic, exciting, colorful sea life. You swim with wonder and amazement among beautiful fish and water life, and feel reverence for their unique existence. You have no problem losing awareness, because you are so close to these wondrous beings. You experience no distraction at all as your attention is entirely on what's around and in front of you. You drop all ideas and concerns of self.

Visiting an aquarium brings us close to the same exotic sea life. But there is a separation, as if we're in two different worlds. Standing on the other side of the glass, we cannot be intimate with the fish the way we are when we're immersed in the ocean water with them. So we may have interest without excitement, and our awareness can stray.

Not everything in life is emotionally exciting as snorkeling among tropical fish. But excitement isn't the point; excitement come and goes, temporarily satisfying the mind. The point is to experience things fully and continuously, just as they are, ordinary or exotic. Then we can experience intimacy and oneness with everything.

> In a famous Zen koan, Zhaozhou asks Nanquan, "What is the Way?"
>
> Nansen answered, "Ordinary mind is the Way."
>
> Zhaozhou asked, "Shall I try to seek after it?"
>
> Nanquan responded, "If you try for it, you will become separated from it."
>
> Zhaozhou continued to push for something concrete: "How can I know the Way unless I try for it?"
>
> Nanquan said, "The Way is not a matter of knowing or not knowing. Knowing is delusion; not knowing is confusion."[14]

The meaning of the koan is to feel and experience the transcendent and universal in the things of everyday life, rather than pursuing it or thinking about it. Thirteenth-century Zen master Wumen commented on this koan:

> The spring flowers, the autumn moon;
> Summer breezes, winter snow.
> If useless things do not clutter your mind,
> You have the best days of your life
> So when our awareness is fully alive, ordinary things will inspire our practice, just as the fish touches our heart.

Suzuki Roshi told this story about stone gathering in Japan:

In the spring after a big rain or flood, the creek becomes clear so that the stones at the bottom can be seen easily. People then like to collect them for their gardens. It is a big event; everyone brings a picnic. The people who go on ahead of others usually don't find best stones. The last person who does get excited—who listens to the birds and sees running stream without actually searching for the best stone, by chance finds the best stone. The person who goes ahead of the others is known as "chicken eyes," always seeking and scratching for something to have. His mind is too small and too busy, always looking around, not seeing anything. But everyday mind is always finding something good.

CLEARING AWAY MIND ASHES

Guishan was an influential teacher in the Zen tradition. He lived in China in the late eighth and early ninth centuries. He and his disciple Yaoshan founded the first school of Zen, the Guiyang school. Guishan's teacher was Baizhang.

One day when Guishan was visiting his teacher, Baizhang said, "Guishan, check the stove to see if there is any fire." Guishan looked and said, "No, the fire is out." Baizhang got up and poked around in the ashes and found an ember. He showed it to Kuei Shan and said, "Is this not fire?" At that moment, Guishan was enlightened.[15]

Guishan could not see the ember because his own mind was like ash. Baizhang knew that Guishan's true nature was hidden like the ember, so he showed him the ember that existed in the ashes. Before that, Guishan didn't know his true nature. Baizhang took the opportunity to show how ashes in the mind can hide our true nature.

When we see only the ashes of our mind, we can't recognize our true self; we are not aware of our true nature. Baizhang demonstrated that we must set aside our delusional, distracted notions to let the spark of our true nature appear.

To live a happy, confident life, we don't have to worry about images of ourself. We give up displaying or protecting an image. Most of us spend our lives carrying around some image of ourself, trying hard to craft it, display it, and defend it. When we do this, we create ashes. Stuck with an image of ourself, we create more and more ashes and cannot feel the glow of our true self. We let mind ashes hide our true nature, just as if we are hiding from ourself, and hiding from each other.

In zazen practice, we clear away the ashes. We sit with no idea of creating or protecting an image. We just sit quietly, aware of our breath, willing to let go of any thoughts that appear. Then the ember of our true self becomes clear to us and we feel warmed by it. And we have no further need for a made-up image.

When we are young, we need to be motivated to learn how to do things, to take care of ourselves and have a creative life. Children's motivation comes from outside. Parents push children to school and teach them to behave in certain ways. Athletic coaches push their athletes to practice and be good teammates. Most young people need motivation from outside themselves. When we are adults, motivation is supposed to come from within. The usual belief is that we need a personal, internal goal that will encourage us to make our best effort. But if that goal is based on ashes, we won't have a stable life even if we achieve it.

There's no joy in our life if our motivation comes from the ashes of ego. The most effective way is to be motivated by our true nature. Neither from outside or inside, but from the glowing ember of our true self. Our true nature does not need motivation. It's always ready to express itself, to create or take care of something. So we just let ourself be motivated by our true nature.

Our attitude should be like both Baizhang and Guishan,

teacher and student. One understands without doubt that the ember is there, glowing continuously. Baizhang always has his eye on the ember; seeing past ashes. At the same time, we need to have the mind of Guishan, who is ready to be shown, ready to see, ready to set aside ashes to have his true nature appear. We should always be teacher and student for ourselves and each other.

Our thinking mind is magnificent in the ways it creates ideas and stores knowledge. But when it creates and stores ideas about itself, our thinking becomes heavy, laden down with ash. Then, our mind feels heavy from overthinking. So, Buddhism advises, "Put aside your thinking mind, especially when it comes to yourself." Otherwise, our mood will become heavy, and we'll be joyless, careless, and uncaring.

The free mind is empty of images of itself. It is light, clear, without exaggerations or prejudices. This is Original Mind. The greatest enlightenment is nothing but daily life itself, lived without the mind being weighed down by images of itself. That is why we say, "Mind is Buddha."

But it is difficult to detach from images of ourself, because it's become a habit. We feel that it is necessary to create and display an image of ourself. But even if we are successful in maintaining that image, it will not be a source of peace, joy, or stability. Zazen practice is the way we learn to let go of false images. It's how we push aside the ash and stop creating new ash. In zazen, we are warmed by the embers of our true self and learn how it glows continuously. And because of the warmth of these embers, we find the lightness of life.

10

BEYOND INSPIRATION

I STARTED MY Zen practice many years ago, inspired by a story about Yunmen, a well-known master in ninth-century China. He once said, "Our school lets you go any way you like. It kills and it brings to life either way."[16] In the assembly that night, one of the monks asked, "How does it kill?" Mater Yunmen replied, "Winter goes, and spring comes." Then the monk asked, "How is it when winter goes and spring comes?" And Yunmen said, "Shouldering a staff, you wander this way and that, East or West, North or South, knocking at the wild stumps as you please."[17]

I didn't understand the meaning or the metaphors from ninth-century China, but I felt a great sense of freedom reading that story. Even though I couldn't relate it to my life directly, I felt inspired and then I thought, what do I do with this inspiration? I had no idea what to do next, or if there even was a next step. So I continued reading Zen books and talking about them with friends at work in hallway conversations. Then, some years later, I met Suzuki Roshi and started Zen practice.

I was profoundly inspired by him, by his way, but I was confused by his lectures and what he might be trying to say. And I was confused by zazen practice: "What is this uncomfortable posture? What am I supposed to *do*?" But because I felt inspired, I continued my practice. I watched Suzuki Roshi—his ways and how he was with people—and I realized that was the answer to "What's next?"

It was the early 1960s, a lifetime ago for many of you, and the Zen students at that time were very casual about their practice. To me, they did not appear to be bringing their practice to their daily life. There was a lot of carelessness, rudeness, drugs, and sex. But Suzuki Roshi accepted every one of them without reservation or criticism. I, in turn, judged them for their attitudes and their behavior. And I thought, how can he accept them without saying a word? Then I realized I was judging him for not judging them. Even though I was inspired by his gentle, non-judging way, that was not enough for me to be gentle and nonjudgmental. And when I saw that about myself, it was a revelation. I'd never seen myself that way before.

In life, there are many potential sources of inspiration. We have books, lectures, classes, retreats, videos, podcasts, movies, and many more ways that may inspire us. We might also have personal encounters with inspired people. But how do we go from feeling inspired to *becoming* what that inspiration points to? This is one of the big questions that arises during our practice. What does it mean to be truly inspired, not just for the moment, a week, or a month, but within us? We need to ask, "Is this feeling of inspiration always alive in my life?"

Inspiration can animate our life when it guides us to action, when it's not just something we feel good about but something that will create change or make things better. Inspiration activates us to make things better socially, politically, and in our work, things that are personal and private and in all our relationships.

But for inspiration to really move us, we have to be expanded and broadened beyond our ordinary life. We have to feel that our life is deeper than how we live and what we experience in daily life. To be inspired, *we have to wake up to ourselves*. There can be no lasting inspiration in our life if we are not awake—to ourselves, to what we're doing, and to how we're doing it.

For inspiration to work through us, it has to become deeper than the surface excitement we feel. To inspire every moment, it has to seep into our marrow so we can commit to whatever changes we have to make, break habits when we see they are harmful, commit to new ways of being when we see that would be helpful, start to have a new attitude when we see that we must, and commit to a change in a relationship if we see it's for the better. This is the work of our daily life.

To make these changes requires work, adjustments, and sacrifice, some of which can be painful. To bring real inspiration into our lives we need to look at ourselves honestly and let go of some long-held habits. But with inspiration and discipline, we can change.

Ultimately, inspiration doesn't come from the outside. We can't rely on external inspiration for our freedom. That would be like living from vacation to vacation, from one excitement to the next, always waiting for the next inspiring word or special event to get us through. If we do this, we'll spend the rest of our life waiting for life to appear. We shouldn't mistake a single inspiration, exciting and joyous as it may be, for real life. Only through diligent effort can inspiration be deep enough to see how things really are and how our own life can be.

Inspiration must go from the words we hear or read, and from ideas and emotions, to a vision, a feeling of certainty of how we want to be in the world and what we want to express with our life. Reading stories about spiritual teachers and what they said and did, we may be inspired and even excited. The stories of ancient times can illustrate their effort facing difficulties in order to bring inspiration deeply into their lives—by looking into their own lives and their own karma.

The Buddha, until he was in his mid-twenties, lived a comfortable, privileged life as a prince destined to become king. All his desires were taken care of. But one day he got a glimpse of old age, illness, death, and suffering, and he embarked on years of hard practice, which he continued for the rest of his life. He was inspired by what he saw, and he was ready.

Dogen's mother died when he was eight years old. At her funeral, he saw the smoke from the incense rising and he was immediately struck by the transiency of life. So he became a monk and went on many long journeys in search of truth.

Suzuki Roshi admits that he made many painful mistakes, but he kept going, even into areas that were unfamiliar to him. He also had a vision and was inspired by what he wanted to do. These teachers and others were determined to explore their inspirations and come to some understanding. In acknowledging difficulties he encountered following an inspiration, Suzuki Roshi said, "For a Zen student, a weed is a treasure."[18]

Usually, we hear something inspiring, but we don't follow through. We don't know what to do with it. The initial inspiration comes as a gift in the colorful wrapping of emotional excitement. We need to put that wrapping aside to get to the heart of the inspiration, to what moves us. We need to ask ourselves, beyond the wrapping, what else is here? It's the same as asking, what's in me? To follow our inspiration, we have to ask, who am I?

In this practice, we start by giving up our addiction to emotional excitement, which is a lot of what activates our current world. One excitement after the other and we become addicted to them, to having more of them and having them continuously. We need to give up that addiction and look for something else to provide us with inspiration, otherwise we are like addicts looking for a fix, hoping for a temporary relief from our karmic burden. If we're interested only in isolated inspirational moments, we will stay captive to our habits, our reactions, and that patterns that have been developed from our life history of difficulties and painful experiences.

True inspiration means making the effort to break the habits by going beyond the wrapping paper and opening the box containing our delusions, mistakes, fears, and disgraces. Suzuki Roshi once said, "You have to go back to the source of your karma."

So, when we feel inspired by something that we see or hear, we should look at *why* we feel inspired. Why did I feel a sense of liberation from that event or those words? And what is it about myself that prevents my freedom?

We are the ones who prevent our own freedom. When we look at our karma, we may not like what we find: painful memories, horrendous mistakes. But if we recognize the universal nature of our painful moments, we can turn them into treasures. As Dogen writes at the end of Genjokoan ("The Actualization of Englightenment"): "The wind of Buddhism makes the earth golden and causes the rivers to flow with sweet, fermented milk."[19]

11

THE PURSUIT OF HAPPINESS

THE PURSUIT OF happiness is a founding principle of the United States Constitution. And this idea is embedded in our country's fabric and in people's minds. But when we look at "the pursuit of happiness" through the eyes of Zen practice, we see that happiness is not something you can actually pursue. You can't hold it in your hands or store it on a shelf. Happiness is not a commodity or something you can possess. You cannot buy happiness.

The problem is, we see the world as primarily composed of material things, and in our minds, this makes perfect sense. Almost everything in our everyday lives is physical. But when we begin to experience our lives through *the mind of practice*, we see that materiality is just one dimension. And we come to understand in our gut that we can engage in the world at other levels. We live in a multidimensional world, and holding to an attitude of pursuing a narrow idea of happiness is actually the basis for unhappiness. When we see this world as one-dimensional and hold happiness as our goal, we miss the mark.

The notion of *pursuing* is like seeing the world as though it were made up of toys. We think the world is something to be played with, in the way children play at a playground. When we pursue happiness as something we can possess as if it is a material thing, life itself becomes a toy—a personal toy—and that, of course, is a big misunderstanding of what life is.

Interest in Zen practice in the West started in the 1950s and '60s, and in those early days, the real significance of practice was not understood. It was embraced by hippies, academics, and philosophers, but not the wider population. In those days, Zen was exciting to talk and read about, and practice was seen as a way to get something—the pursuit of enlightenment, fame, or recognition, or something you could talk about at parties. Practicing Zen was a way of standing out. It was a kind of toy or a work of art imported from China or Japan, like having a statue of the Buddha in your garden or a calligraphy scroll on the wall of your home. Zen was something to possess.

But over time as people got serious about the practice it began to be recognized as a profound way to understand and live our lives. We came to see practice as having the power to clarify the meaning of our life and put an end to confusion.

As we continue to engage in the practice, it's important to know what it is at its core. It's more than just following instructions or mechanically doing what your teacher tells you. And it's not enough to think, "I've begun to practice and I know what I'm doing, or even to tell your friends, 'I'm a Zen student.'" When we practice that way or pose as somebody special, we're just creating a new image of ourselves. We're playing with Zen as though it's a toy.

Children love comic book heroes. They're portraits of courage and selflessness, dedicated to fighting injustice. Kids dress up as their heroes and imitate them, and these figures provide models of behavior they can admire. When they pay attention to comic book heroes and even dress like them, it's a way of practicing some of the best qualities of being an adult. But of course, when they become adults, dressing up as comic book heroes is not generally helpful. To mature means to grow out of pretending, fantasizing, or posing. To mature means to put aside our toys and integrate these admirable qualities into our own lives.

When we start Zen practice, it does feel as if we're pursuing something like enlightenment or increased mental power, understanding or peace of mind, which we desperately need. It's natural to have this understanding when we begin; but at some point, it is important to realize that Zen practice is not a pursuit. It's a way to take care of ourselves, which includes being kind and generous to ourselves and others so we will have a relaxed, confident, and warm sense about our life.

Our practice includes cultivating a taking-care attitude. This is the best gift we can give ourselves, and it extends to our daily life and to others. Siddhartha Gautama, who became the Buddha, was the son of a chieftain, something like a king. Siddhartha was intelligent, handsome, and talented. He and his family led a privileged life. Despite all this, as the legend tells us, the young man found palace life with its petty tasks and amusements to be constricting. He found little pleasure in the luxury and affluence around him, and yearned for freedom and a broader and deeper life. He understood that life is not a toy.

One night he and his attendant snuck out of the palace so Siddhartha could see the world outside the palace walls— the everyday lives of ordinary people. As the story tells us, he encountered various forms of suffering. He saw someone who was sick and realized that many people were sick and there were few cures for these diseases (in those days). He saw an elderly man and understood that aging is relentless and there is no turning back to a younger time. And he saw a dying man and realized that when death visits upon us, there is no going back.

After that, the prince who was to become Buddha saw a monk in a yellow robe who had few possessions but seemed calm and joyful. He was continuously smiling and seemed untroubled. Prince Siddhartha knew immediately that he wanted to be like that, free from suffering in the largest sense, and for that he was willing to give up his privileges. Giving up wealth may be easy. We can adjust to a life with fewer comforts. But it's difficult to give up privilege, to give up your sense of entitlement.

To give up the privileges of royalty, of being in charge and able to do what you want whenever you want, is a big act. Not long after, Siddhartha left his comfortable home and went on pilgrimage, seeking understanding and a way out of suffering. In doing so, he gave up his privileges. Leaving home and going on a solitary pilgrimage was not unusual in the Buddha's day. That lifestyle was recognized as valid and noble.

We all yearn for happiness. We want to be satisfied with our lives, whatever that may mean for us. Sometimes we feel that material things will make us happy. Sometimes we need positive emotions. This young man who was to become a Buddha had both, but it wasn't enough. He knew something was missing, something intangible beyond personal possessions and good feelings, something his thinking mind could not reach. So he sought the intangible through the practice of his day, which was to leave home.

After a number of years of effort, encountering difficulties and frustration, he had a profound insight. He understood that there is no need to pursue it, whatever *it* is, and that he and all creatures already have it. He discovered that wisdom is always present; we are always in the midst of it. Why do we work so hard to uncover the wisdom that's already here? Why don't we recognize that we already have it? The answer comes to us through our practice, and that answer is that the mind is too busy *pursuing* to see that "it" is right in front of us.

The foundation of our practice is to stop our physical and

mental activities for a time and let our mind be as still as a pond with no ripples. Only then can we see what is going on beneath the surface. Most of us cannot live in monasteries or as wanderers like the monk the Buddha saw outside his palace. This lifestyle is not viable for many of us, and we don't want to be secluded. But we can have a monk's mind, a monk's attitude, and a monk-like practice when we sit on our cushions and throughout our daily life. And we can say to ourselves, *stop pursuing*. We do this as a reminder that there's no need to pursue anything.

When our practice isn't strong yet, we may need to be strict with ourselves, and reminders can help. The point of a reminder is not to criticize or scold ourselves or follow the precepts of the Buddha too rigidly.

We already have the most important thing in our life. Pursuing something else and attaching to the various things of our life is a recipe for unhappiness. We can end the confusion around the pursuit of happiness by mindfully taking care of what is fundamental in our life as it is. Zazen is a good starting place, attending to our physical posture and our mind, and it continues in our relationships with everyone and everything. We have everything we need, and we are always *with* it all. When we stop trying to add things, even happiness, and stop being anxious about what we don't have, we will be satisfied—and happy—to be here right now and to take care of ourselves and everyone with a calm and gentle mind.

12

WALKING PAST THE CANDY STORE

THE GREATEST OBSTACLES to spiritual practice are our expectations—our desire to gain something for ourself from our effort. Trying to gain anything only hinders our practice, even if we believe that what we want is unselfish.

We come to practice because of some angst or confusion about life's meaning. We have questions about how to live, about right effort and right livelihood. We start to practice because we've been feeling unsatisfied in our daily activities, troubled by various feelings and emotions. We want our practice to show us what direction our life should take, to resolve our confusion and bring us peace of mind. We begin to sit with that expectation. But if peace of mind is a goal—and if we pursue it—we cannot attain it. Our confusion will not be resolved.

Suzuki Roshi used to talk about candy. He warned us not to seek "candy" from Zen practice. He said that practice should be pure and natural, that it should not have what he called a "gaining idea." We should practice without an idea of obtaining "candy" for our mind, even peace of mind. Pure, deep practice can only happen when we do not expect candy of any kind, in any form.

Suzuki Roshi said, "Enlightenment is just candy," admitting

that this may seem blasphemous. He added that the point of Zen practice is not to gain some experience and that true enlightenment is not some extraordinary incident.[20] In contrast to the usual view of practice, he said that if we feel or understand something, that is not true enlightenment. True enlightenment, he said, is to go beyond ourselves, beyond ideas of who we are, beyond ideas of practice, and of what we feel we must have.

The point he tried to make is that we should practice without expecting anything special for ourselves, even enlightenment or peace of mind. Any expectation is a desire, and any desire is an obstacle to practice, even if it does not seem selfish or harmful. We might as well try to obtain fame, fortune, or magical powers. All are just different flavors of "candy."

How do we learn to practice without desire? We begin by devoting ourself to our practice, developing continuous practice. We shouldn't think, maybe I'll continue, maybe I won't; let's see how I feel. Such an idea is about our self and is a form of candy. Our mind creates attractive wrappings for candy. We shouldn't be fooled by fancy wrappings.

In his *Treasury of the True Dharma Eye* fascicle, "Gyoji, Continuous Practice," Dogen describes how Huike, the second patriarch in China, underwent self-imposed hardships to be accepted as a disciple by Bodhidharma. When Bodhidharma encountered Huike standing all night in the snow, he told Huike, "The way of the Buddhas and patriarchs is based on patience. The most difficult practice is ceaseless practice. If you have only a small amount of virtue and wisdom and try to seek the true teaching, you will feel only suffering and the results will be useless."[21]

"The most difficult practice is ceaseless practice" means that our mind is easily distracted by ideas of candy and caught by desire. In our practice, we are determined to have practice continuously, and we acknowledge our desires. In other words, we are aware when we're looking in the window of the candy store. The practice is to keep walking one step at a time, past many exciting candy stores on both sides of the street. It's not that we never visit exciting stores and enjoy things we find exciting. But we avoid ideas like "I want excitement" or "I'm not enjoying this." We simply engage our self in whatever we are doing.

To have pure practice is to have no ideas about practice. Before notions of "pure" and "impure," "enjoying" or "not enjoying," even before ideas about life or the purpose of practice, we practice. Especially, we should have no idea about "what I will get if I practice."

Zazen helps us see how much we like candy. Zen practice invites us, instead, to taste the deliciousness of ordinary life.

13

EXPLORING THE TERRITORY

IF YOU PRACTICE Zen continuously and with dedication, the landscape of your life will expand and you will uncover areas within you that you haven't explored before. These will probably include difficulties, and because of your practice they will surface and you'll have to face them. In Zen practice, we have to travel our own path and discover for ourselves the obstacles along the way.

These challenges are not on a map. No one else can point them out to us. In today's world, speed and efficiency are highly valued. We try to master things as quickly as possible. But in Zen practice, efficiency won't help us much, because self-discoveries reveal themselves at their own pace, and it's usually a slow and steady process.

When a problem appears, we have to explore for ourselves what we mean by "a problem appears." We explore the so-called problem to understand it and determine what to do. Similarly, we need to explore when "no problem appears," and to explore "Buddha Nature" and "Enlightenment." With this slow, steady exploration, we will develop a subtle and refined attitude toward our life and we will appreciate things just as they are from the depth of our wisdom, not through our intellect. If you

56   Les Kaye

are taught something by someone, you might appreciate and embrace it, but you might not really understand it when you simply accept what someone else tells you.

In our practice, without our own effort to understand, we may lose this flexibility of mind, but when our attitude emphasizes this process of discovery, our true nature is fully active.

There is a story about a man who is in bed at night, half-asleep, and is searching with his hand for his pillow. He can't see anything but he is actively seeking. When things aren't clear in front of us but we are actively seeking, our mind is fully engaged. If we know where our pillow is, there's no need to search for it, and that's okay. But in that situation, the mind is acting in a limited way. But if we don't know where it is, our mind is open and alert and we will be able to make many discoveries. If we think we've attained some goal, we might stop seeking and stop practicing. Any satisfaction we feel based on attainment is temporary. On the other hand, a mind that is continuously seeking feels satisfaction, understanding, and freedom.

Exploring your body and mind through your own effort is the most important practice, cultivating a seeking attitude that brings a wider understanding. And through this exploration, you will discover your capacity of understanding all things. Then, whatever you do, whether you achieve a goal or not, is a good use of time. But when you do something based on a limited idea or for the purpose of attainment, you may gain something concrete or very useful, but it will not encourage your Buddha nature.

Suzuki Roshi called this our "Way-Seeking Mind"—seeing things with a wide viewpoint, especially in the midst of our fluid world. Our usual tendency is to explore the things we believe will make us feel good, and to ignore the things we don't like. This attitude is narrow and self-oriented, and it

I Had a Good Teacher   57

limits our power to explore things, and it becomes difficult to understand what is truly important.

For example, if you lose an election, you might say it's a bad thing and not want to look at it. But if we don't explore it, we won't learn anything. We won't know how to do better next time. When we ignore the things we don't like, we become narrow. We need to have humility so we will explore not just what we like. We need to have an attitude that encourages us to explore what we like, and what we don't like. And we need to find out why we think that something is good or something else is bad. If we are always looking for what is good, we will limit our capacity and we will limit the terrain of our world.

Suzuki Roshi rarely explained anything in detail. The best way to learn from him was to eat with him, to watch him, to work with him, and also to help him without being told how to help. When we wanted to help him, we paid careful attention to discover how to help. He rarely scolded people, and when he did it often was not clear why. We had to make an effort to find out. This is the spirit of our practice.

He told the story of being scolded by his teacher as a young student at Eihei-ji Monastery. He was his teacher's attendant, serving tea and performing other chores. One day he opened the sliding door to offer his teacher some tea. In Japan, you slide the left door to the right and the right door to the left. He slid the door from the left, and he was scolded without understanding why. Later he saw a small round hole in the right screen door and realized that's where you put your finger to slide the door open. From that moment on, he always opened the door from the right.

But one morning when he opened the door from the right, he was scolded again: "Not that side!" At first, he didn't understand, but then he realized that his teacher had a guest who was sitting on that side, and he realized that you open the door on the side where the guest is not seated. He had to discover the rules by himself.

Each of us is unique. There is not one way for everybody. We each have our own, and yet, we have to adjust our way to find the most appropriate response to each particular situation. What is important is not to stick to any one way, but to find out what is appropriate right now. If you are in the temple and the work leader says, "Today we're going to clean windows," you see the box of rags and it turns out that there are more people than rags, so you think, I guess there's nothing for me to do. But that is not the attitude of Zen practice, which is to look at the overall situation, explore what is going on, and find a way to help. Even when we are given rules, they may not be hard and fast, so we try to be flexible.

But sometimes, we need hard and fast rules, like obeying traffic lights. Because of rules like these, when strictly followed, we're able to share the road safely. When there is a need for rules, we may need to establish a rule for harmony, so it becomes easy to say, "Well, this is the rule. This is how we should always do it." But that too is not our way of practicing.

The best way to teach people is closely, one on one, but sometimes that's not possible. We need general instructions for everyone. But we shouldn't stick to the words. We need to think deeply about the real meaning of a rule. For beginners, instructions are needed, but experienced students can find their own way with fewer instructions. Instructions are a starting point, but we need to go beyond instructions to discover what's appropriate. We don't emphasize a fixed, literal meaning. True study of the Way of practice means making an effort to stay open and finding out whether what we think turns out to be correct or not.

A small child who has a crayon and paper will draw something without thinking whether it's good or bad. Sometimes we have to do things in that way, not knowing why. If we find that too difficult and insist on knowing the reason, if we have too much resistance, zazen will be very difficult. We have to surrender to doing what we have to do, even though there is nothing to surrender to. If you don't understand, that's okay. Please find out for yourself.

14

LIFE IS PERFECT

Mᴏʀᴇ ᴛʜᴀɴ ᴀ thousand years ago during the Golden Age of Zen in China, a man was walking from his village to another, and he had to pass through a forest. When he entered the forest, he saw a tiger looking at him from the underbrush, and he began to walk faster. Then he heard the tiger running behind him and began to run for his life. Quickly, he came to the edge of a cliff, and he grabbed hold of a vine and slowly stepped down onto a ledge just as the tiger caught up with him. Hanging over the side of the cliff clutching the vine, the tiger pacing above him, the man looked down and saw another tiger below. At that moment, a mouse came out from a crack in the side of the cliff and began chewing on the very vine he was holding. The man then noticed a patch of wild strawberries growing from a clump of earth, and with his free hand, reached out and picked a strawberry. It was plump and perfectly ripe, warmed by the sun. He put the strawberry in his mouth and, savoring the flavors, exclaimed, "How delicious!"

Zen stories like this are designed to wake us up to the fundamental truth that *life is perfect* and cannot be more perfect than it is right now. We mostly overlook this; our distracted mind keeps this insight out of reach. When you practice zazen in the morning and a bird's song enters your quiet mind, it goes straight to your heart. That's a gift of the present moment, and it's perfect. It would be foolish to think, I wish it were a different bird! When you accept that birdsong, or any sound, without thinking, you will feel the power of practice. In our practice, *life is perfect in each moment.* This is true even when it doesn't feel perfect, even when we're drowning in problems or surrounded by tigers. Somewhere in us, we know that life is perfect, regardless of how we feel. Each present moment is complete, and there's no separation, no room for imperfection. When you practice zazen continuously, you will feel this truth.

Daily life is complex and difficult. It was so in ancient times and it is true today. Most moments don't actually feel perfect because we're unconsciously pursuing our *ideas* of perfection, comparing the present moment to an image of what we want this moment to be. Our image may include comfort, love, safety, wealth, or status, the things human beings yearn for. But when we strive, we overlook our inherent perfection. We feel that something is missing, and the moment is not perfect, but it is. Each moment is perfect despite whatever we feel is missing.

We enter spiritual practice from a place of uncertainty. We feel we're not in tune with life. We're out of sync with something we can't put our finger on. So we respond to this feeling of dissatisfaction by striving—to gain things, to collect things—with the idea that this will fill our emptiness. But in Zen practice, we learn to go *beyond collecting and beyond a feeling of separation.* We have everything we need. When we put an end to striving, we feel a sense of oneness.

Millions of Americans don't feel there is anything or anyone they can trust. They feel no one is looking out for them, and they don't feel connected with the whole in a social or a spiritual sense. When we don't feel connected, we become anxious and create ideas about perfection and imperfection, about life and death. Our mind's activity has us longing for perfection and clinging to life, and we reject what's not perfect and we fear death. But through practice, we come to understand that these are ideas created out of anxious feelings. The point of our practice is to recognize the inherent unity, which is our true nature. We practice being mindful continuously and letting the activity of each moment express itself fully, staying fully engaged without ideas of perfect or imperfect.

When we see a flower in bloom, we may say, "Isn't it perfect?" But when the flower starts to wilt and turn brown, is it less perfect? And when the petals begin to fall, does it become not perfect at all? The flower is always perfect. The flower is always the flower completely, moment after moment. The vibrant green leaves and colorful petals are the flower. The brown and decaying petals are also the flower. And the flower that has fallen is the flower, too. When the flower is thriving, we say, "This is life." When it has decayed and is on the ground, even if we say "death," the flower is still the flower. There's no need to worry about birth and death. They are just ideas, different names we give the present moment. There is no separation between life and death. This present moment is life, and this present moment is death. In fact, this moment is independent of what we call it. It is inherently nameless, complete in itself, and it includes everything, the perfect and the imperfect. This inclusivity is why we call it perfect.

Talking this way is easy. It is like discussing philosophy or a theory in a class or a workshop. But we can't appreciate the truth of this moment by talking. We have to practice zazen continuously to feel the subtle wisdom of it. In our practice, we let our busy minds come to rest and allow our body and mind to feel oneness. When we let go of ideas of perfect and not perfect and recognize the sameness of life and death, we can understand the perfection of each moment and the perfect life we have.

We will always have difficulties in life. There will always be tigers around us. It's the nature of being alive. We struggle to survive. We struggle to allow life to continue, but it does not mean we have to suffer. When we know the meaning of our struggles and the relationship of our struggles to our daily life, we won't suffer. Even when we have serious difficulties, it doesn't make life imperfect. We only suffer when we struggle against struggling, and when we think struggling isn't also perfect. When we don't see that life is death and death is life—just different names—we'll have to struggle. We are always born and we are always dying. Life is the continuous presence of struggles, the continuous occurrence of birth and death, moment by moment, and that is why life is perfect in its activity.

15

AFFIRMATION

At the end of a lecture, somebody asked, "How shall I respond to a mentally ill person?" I knew it wasn't a medical question, inquiring about therapies or medicines that might be effective treatment for a troubled individual. It was a religious question, asking me how to relate to an unhappy person. If our attitude is one of caring, the first step would be to reframe the question so we avoid labels that can isolate and stigmatize, and are hard to remove. From a spiritual perspective, the question becomes, *"How do we respond when someone is out of harmony?"* The answer, as I see it, is to respond as a mother would to her baby.

Infants disrupt our routines with their constant needs and demands and their inability to take care of themselves. A caring mother doesn't isolate her child out of frustration or impatience; she instinctively knows how unnatural that would be and how it would lead to suffering. So, our attitude needs to start with selflessness directed toward someone who is not in harmony. Part of the responsibility we have to each other is the practice of compassion. If our attitude is self-centered, it encourages separation and isolation. If we turn away from someone who is out of balance because we feel uncomfortable or that engaging them is "too much trouble," we create even more disharmony. We need to see whether our orientation is self-centered.

Poet Su Dong Po lived a millennium ago in China. While hiking in the forest, he had a profound awakening, and he wrote: "The sound of the valley stream is his great tongue. The colors of the mountains are his pure body."[22]

Nature, presented by Su Dong Po with human attributes, *affirms our life*. His words express why we love nature and want to be close to it and preserve it. At the same time, Su Dong Po shows that when we as humans affirm nature, our life affirms the lives of others and the lives of others affirm our life. Dogen comments, "It is regrettable that many only appreciate the superficial aspects of sound or color." Understanding that our relationships are inherently affirming is the basis for the spiritual life.

We're all out of harmony at times. But most of us have the resilience to come back to balance and continue our lives in relative harmony. Others may be less fortunate. Harmony eludes them, and they spend much of their lives in isolation. *Our practice is to affirm life as we meet it.* When we feel isolated, we can try to encourage harmony. If we don't know what to do, we experiment, intuitively trying *something*. And when we're upset, we can quiet our mind and return to balance.

Dogen wrote:

> To learn the Buddhist way is to learn about oneself.
> To learn about oneself is to forget oneself.
> To forget oneself is to perceive oneself as all things.[23]

In other words, we are affirmed by all things, and by extension, all things are affirming all things. And this affirmation is continuously active, continuously practicing like mountains and rivers, aware of what is going on.

Chan master Guo Jun Fashi wrote:

Sitting itself will not give you enlightenment.
Meditation will not give it to you.
It will only lead you to the brink.
Retreating from the world will not liberate you.
Happiness is not found in a secluded forest or isolated cave.
Enlightenment comes when you connect to the world.
Only when you truly connect with everyone and everything else
Do you become enlightenment.
Only by going deeply and fully into the world do you obtain liberation.[24]

Our practice of bowing to each other (gassho) is an expression of affirmation. We fully connect; we aren't passive or indifferent. By giving up our self in this way, we discover the joy of being with the other person, without concern for like or dislike. As Suzuki Roshi said, "Sometimes we bow to cats and dogs." In the same way, we should be ready to bow to everyone.

Sitting in meditation with others is an act of affirming each other, with acceptance and without judgment. Being together helps dissolve any sense of isolation, a problem of the modern world. Great benefits have come into to our lives through technology, but in our excitement to embrace it, we don't recognize how it can isolate us. We have to reflect on how to use technology, consider when and where to use it—and its value in that moment, measured against its impact on our relationships with each other. In the same way, we should reflect on how to use our life. Are we encouraging harmony or isolation? Are we active in the continual affirmation of all things?

When we meet a difficult or out-of-balance person, our practice and our inherent nature demand that we become spiritually creative and find ways to affirm them as the starting point of taking care.

THE SOUP OF OUR LIFE

I HOPE THAT all young children, at some time in their childhood, have a chance to fly a kite. What keeps a kite stable is the tail. It allows the kite to flow gracefully with the currents. If you try to fly a kite without a tail, it crashes. We could say that a kite without its tail is not at peace.

Our world is full of kites. Each of us and everybody and everything in the world is like a kite trying to flow gracefully. And we come across kites without tails every day—people who are not stable, who don't have control of their lives and are unable to stay aloft. They crash. Sometimes our own life feels unstable. Sometimes we feel out of control, pushed about by the winds of change. When that out-of-control, unstable feeling gets too strong, we look for a place of stability. We want to be at peace.

We may seek a church or a Zen center or a psychotherapist. Or we may adhere to a belief system or connect with someone wise—someone who will ground us and bring us stability. But seeking support is just the start. It usually takes a non-trivial learning experience to learn to rely on ourselves, to discover that the center of our world is not outside us. Nor is there a single fixed point within, material or a fixed set of beliefs. It's more like a centripetal force pulling our body and mind inward. But a more useful image for practice might be that of making soup.

When we cook a pot of soup, there's no center, no single focal point. We focus on all the ingredients and see how they affect each other and what they create together. If we make a minestrone with all its ingredients, each spoonful is full of life. There may be pasta in the first bite, a vegetable in the next, then a tomato comes up, and then some beans. Our pot of soup has no one center; it embraces all the ingredients and flavors and they flow together easily.

We want to live life the way we make a soup. Each moment is a new experience, and all are interrelated and supportive of each other. We need all the ingredients. If we prepare a soup carelessly, we won't be able to enjoy the ingredients. If we don't prepare it mindfully, it might taste strange or even burn. We need to pay attention.

If we don't bring a caring attitude into all aspects of our life, some experiences won't be nourishing. Some may even become a burden, an ingredient that's not pleasant to the palate. So, we prepare ourselves moment by moment with a mind of generosity, a mind that doesn't hold back. This is the mind of enlightenment we are seeking, but we get too wrapped up in our seeking and don't recognize what we're looking for, even when it shows up on our kitchen table. It's not outside yourself. It's you—your original generous mind.

The moment the mind is ready to give generously, that is the mind of stability. The world is always changing and we're always having new experiences. These are the ingredients of life, but when we have a mind of giving, we ourselves stay centered.

We come to the practice because of difficult experiences— sad or frightening. We call it "suffering." But with a mind of giving, no suffering arises out of difficulties. Only when our mind is not generous will the difficulties that we encounter make us anxious. A mind that is oriented toward itself is always at risk of sadness, fear, shame, and anger. But when we are not afraid of losing our possessions, our mind will always be stable. That mind understands that there's nothing to lose, no such thing as having to give up something. There is only giving. A mind of giving is open and receptive to whatever unfolds. When we don't have that receptivity to the things that occur in our life, it can feel like a prison. We can't find a way out.

In our practice, we don't talk much about enlightenment. Instead, we talk about the joy of letting go, the mind of giving, and the mind of non-attachment. When we have that kind of mind, we're able to live wisely. Enlightenment is relating wisely to the things of the world—our friends, our homes, our family, and our possessions. Acting wisely and not possessively, we can relate generously. Or we stay attached to things and act unwisely in our life. Nothing in the everyday world is ours to keep. Everything is a gift to be shared.

There is a well-known story of a monk in China who lived in a tiny hut as a hermit with few possessions. One day a thief came and told the monk to give him everything in his hut. The monk said, "Take everything. Help yourself." So, the robber took everything he could find and left. Then the hermit noticed that the thief had overlooked a little bag with some things in it, so he ran after him, shouting, "Wait, you forgot something!" The robber was amazed at the hermit's attitude, and he brought everything back. He apologized and asked the hermit if he could be his student.

The Buddha and his followers lived outside of society, although they related to the everyday world. And centuries later, Dogen and other teachers in China and Japan advocated avoiding worldly affairs altogether. They lived deep in the mountains and stayed away from all that.

The hermit's life in the days of old was one of no attachments. He avoided even the temptation of attachment. By being away from temptation, he was able to cultivate a mind that was calm and stable, because he wasn't holding on to possessions and had no thoughts of success or failure. He had no anxieties about the stuff of the everyday world. And he had peace of mind.

But that was long ago. Few people today can live like a strict Zen hermit. Our practice is to be in the world with others and to learn how to utilize our capacities, create families, be engaged in society, and feel love. If we can't live as an ascetic, we have to find other ways to practice. Having some possessions, we run the risk of feeling possessive or selfish and being anxious about that.

Not dropping out is our challenge. Even while living in a society that emphasizes materialism and possessions, we can cultivate a generous mind. That is the antidote to our karmic difficulties. Our anxieties and stresses and the demands on us all dissolve in the soup of generosity. In the generous mind, there's no anxiety, only readiness. Without generosity, we will always be anxious, always worried. Should I? Shouldn't I? We struggle to be charitable. We struggle to be strong enough to possess very little and to give things away. It's not a trade-off. We don't have to choose between the peace of mind of a hermit or experiences that create anxiety. They can coexist when we include others in our view of the world. This is why Sangha, community, is so important in our practice.

The Sangha is the soup, and we are the ingredients. Is our zendo a spiritual practice place or a community? It's whatever we want it to be. Being generous is not a casual thing. Generosity is a ritual rather than a result of trade-offs, speculation, or payback. It is expressed in our relationships in community, a paradigm of connection and an expression of our true nature. With generosity, we can offer something even greater than ourselves.

17

FINDING YOUR RHYTHM

People's lives today are busy, complicated, and speedy. There's a lot of anxiety in the air. Emotions erupt easily, and people are angry with themselves and others about so many things. This suffering is present in many dimensions of our lives and we need to learn to balance our time and vary our activities so we are not caught in just one way of being.

When we follow the threads of our busy mind, we're likely to become anxious, feeling the pressures we're under. We need to be careful not to let time rule us, and dominate all we have to do. Of course, we need to schedule meetings with others and know when to do this or that activity. But most important is to trust our self to determine where and when and how to be.

Time itself is neutral. When we're thirsty, we don't need to say it's time for a glass of water. We just drink water. Time is a factor in many decisions, but most important is to pay attention to our self and find ways to live in balance. We need to learn not to be a slave to time, to find the freedom to take care of our activities, others, and ourselves, even during days when time seems to be in short supply.

Relaxation techniques can help, and meditation can be

used to relax, reduce stress, and create well-being. Some people tell me that when they don't do zazen in the morning, they miss it and their days don't go as well. But if we focus on meditation as a self-help technique, it's too narrow a focus. Zazen is not a way to achieve something, a technique for attainment or gain. If we do zazen with that kind of attitude, sooner or later we'll become discouraged and quit.

The mindfulness that's very popular these days is often used as a break from our busy days. People get stressed and take meditation breaks. The usual understanding of a break is to disengage, to stop doing what you're doing and rest. Taking a break relieves tension and allows the mind to reflect and feel human again. And zazen can provide these qualities. But our practice has a deeper meaning. At its core it's a way to be deeply present with ourselves and the world, to tune into Big Mind moment after moment, giving us a chance to vary the rhythms of our life.

Whether we are at home or work or school, taking a break means changing the rhythm. It's not to disengage from life. Throughout the day we enter many different rhythms. Some are speedy, some slow, some are excited, some calm, some are hot, and some cold. We need a variety, so we don't get caught in a narrow groove. Without a variety of rhythms, we experience tension overload and we'll burn out.

We engage different rhythms working and walking, chatting and having a cup of tea. These "breaks" are not about disengaging. We continue to stay involved in our life and express our true nature, just with a different rhythm.

The point of our practice is to continue the rhythm of Big Mind, the rhythm of our true nature, which is natural and inherent in us. Big Mind rhythm doesn't change, and it includes all the individual rhythms of our daily life. We'll know how to let our daily life rhythms change when necessary, independent of time. When we do this, whatever we do is continuous practice and an expression of Big Mind, and every task becomes a spiritual activity. We do each thing with the same mindfulness and care.

When we practice without any idea of attaining anything, we become a part of the natural rhythm and know implicitly how to balance our daily activities—what to do and how to do it without anxiety. Our activities become an extension of our practice, and our daily changing rhythms are all in tune, like perfect pitch or a perfect piece of music. When we listen to a great symphony there are individual rhythms throughout, and they change, but the music continues. And we feel the intertwining relationship between the parts and the whole. Doing everything without a gaining idea, with no idea of me or you or activity, we resume our natural rhythm and our effort becomes a beautiful concert.

Zazen practice includes all activities. Like a great piece of music, it brings out the best in all the instruments. Our practice is to continue zazen mind in everything. When we do that, the activities are no trouble. We vary the rhythms and activity of our life easily, and recognize when it's necessary to change the tune. When we want to take a break, it's not just for rest and relief. It's because we know the wisdom of varying the rhythms of our life so we can stay in balance. This is the perspective of practice.

LOVE WITHOUT ATTACHMENT

Love is the most intense feeling we human beings have. Love can make us feel very high and love can make us feel very low. What is the meaning of this love that we think and dream about? The idea of love can be confusing. We think we know what it means—but do we?

Society tells us that love is the most important thing in life. "Love makes the world go 'round." It's the primary force of popular culture—the aspiration for love, ideas of love, the influence of love. Love influences how we dress, the activities we choose, the places we go, and who we associate with. All the things we do are influenced by love, and it's difficult to be happy in life without feeling love.

Love is the main theme in music; and music reflects culture, portraying how a society feels and what's important to it. Country music is about heartbreak; opera emphasizes the loss or the pursuit of love; popular songs are love songs; and most musical genres are about the passion one person feels for another. This consuming passion is at the heart of it all.

When we want love and it's not happening, we become anxious. When we have love and feel loved, we're really happy.

And when we do love but our need is strong and what we have is not enough, we feel dissatisfied.

When we have it and then lose it, we become extremely sad and then angry, and that anger affects our whole life. These emotional ups and downs tell us that love is felt as a personal possession, something outside ourselves to get and hold onto. And we know from Buddhist teachings and practice that the desire to possess only leads to suffering.

As individuals, if we have feelings of love and feel that we are loved, we become a very nice person—generous and friendly, thoughtful, unselfish, and courteous, and we treat everyone around us well, especially the other person. But when we lose the feeling of love, we easily forget about courtesy and generosity and friendliness, and instead feel isolated and rejected. When we experience love in this way—when our state of being depends on whether we feel we have or we don't have love—we are relying on someone else for our fulfillment. This is the way most people live: seeking things in the everyday world that make us feel complete. When love becomes one of these things, we've made it into a commodity. This is not the real meaning of love.

We come to Zen practice when we're tired of pursuing. We've experienced the futility of chasing and relying on things and feelings to satisfy the deepest parts of ourselves. We come because we want our life to be more than the futile efforts at pursuit and never feeling completely satisfied. We come to practice to change our orientation and find a new understanding.

We want to change from pursuing satisfactions that might come to us in the future, to putting our focus on the present moment, a radically different orientation. When we practice, after a while, success in the future becomes less important than simply being present. And being present is not about obtaining a commodity—material or emotional—or achieving a goal. True success is being fully present in this moment. So, the emphasis of Zen practice is not to sacrifice our present life by pursuing a future hope. When we practice, life becomes the continuity of the present moment.

When we don't feel generous, kind, or friendly toward others, we may tell ourselves we'll become a nicer person when we have love, that we need love to feel open to others, which, of course, is a misunderstanding. It's like saying, "When I'm rich, I'll be generous." We don't need riches to be generous, to have a generous mind. And we don't need to possess some commodity to be complete. We are complete without commodities.

Buddhism emphasizes compassion, generosity, and caring. For us to feel this way, it's not up to one person or thing to be the way we want them to be. The usual feeling about love is that it's between two people. But in our practice, love means compassion toward everyone and everything, not just one individual. Compassion is universal, without limits or restrictions. This is true whether some personal desire is satisfied or not.

We can't create a compassionate mind through will alone. Our compassionate nature arises without intervention. When we simply practice, we allow our mind to give up the pursuit of commodities, including love. Practice is about having a limitless mind each moment, which means not sacrificing the present for something that may occur in the future or has occurred in the past. To have limitless mind in each moment, we cannot sacrifice the present. And not sacrificing the present is the foundation of compassion. When we are present, here and now, we can be overflowing with feelings of generosity toward everyone. This is the same mind as being in love, but without the excitement. It is a boundless feeling, a sense of giving ourselves to the world, and allowing the world to possess us—not the other way around.

This giving up is not about losing or surrendering. By giving up pursuing, being in love with the life we have, we gain everything. This is called selflessness and it's the best gift we can give ourselves. It doesn't mean we shouldn't feel love for another person when we feel close to them, only that we should be careful not to let personal love put a limit on us. When our sense of personal love is not possessive, it is universal love.

All feelings and emotions, including love, arise in us because we're human. They are responses to the events and relationships of our life. And like love, other emotions can be very strong too. They can overwhelm our rational mind and affect us physically as well. Like love, they can carry us away, and when we get carried away by any emotion, we're no longer in the present moment. When we are carried away, we become self-oriented, self-centered. We circumscribe our being in the world, and it is in those times that we need to return to awareness, which includes the strong emotions that are there.

In *Zen Mind, Beginner's Mind*, Suzuki Roshi says, "Zen is not some form of excitement."[25] We could say that *authentic* love is not some form of excitement. When we are selfless and compassion arises, the love we feel is universal and has no ups or downs. It's always with us.

THE NATURAL WORLD

More than 2,000 years ago, the Buddha discovered a path to end suffering. Looking at our own lives and the lives of those we love, based on the Buddha's insight, we can see how suffering arises. But if we step back and take a wider view, we see that in the natural world there is no suffering. It simply does not exist. Even though there are hardships, life is in balance. When we live "naturally," we don't feel that there's anything else we need or anything we've lost.

In our everyday lives nowadays, we generate a lot of speed and excitement, and we don't feel connected to nature, the natural world. We have ideas of good and bad, right and wrong, and individually and collectively, we want more things that we feel are special and less of what we find difficult or unpleasant. We collect ideas like this because we think we know what's important, and we even insist on creating a "better" world. But when we can't *feel* the natural world, we can't create a "better" one. Instead, we feel lost, adrift in a sea of competing ideas.

Our practice is to reconnect with the natural world. Suzuki Roshi tells a story about monastery life in Japan. The monks' day-to-day activities are natural—cooking, cleaning, and taking care of things, nothing special. But when visitors come to see the monastery, they take photos of the monks—"unusual people"—to take home as souvenirs, while the monks see the tourists as the unusual ones, taking pictures of them doing their daily routines.

In another story somebody asks the master, "What is your practice?" and the master replies, "When I'm tired, I sleep. When I'm hungry, I eat." In the natural world, we do what we are called to do in each moment. It seems simple, perhaps too simple, almost lazy, like a non-active life with no responsibilities. But in taking care of our work, our jobs, family and friends, we express our creative nature. Whatever presents itself to us in the moment, an impulse to create or to wash the dishes, we take care of it. And when we get tired, we sleep.

Our practice is about paying attention to the flow of the natural world. Dogen wrote:

> Fish in the ocean find the water endless,
> and birds think the sky is without limit.
> However, neither birds nor fish have been separated from their element.
> If birds are separated from their own element, they will die.
> Water is life for fish, the sky is life for birds.
> In the sky, birds are life,
> and in the water, fish are life.[26]

If we become separated from the natural world, we lose the meaning of life and might die. It's important to let go of ideas we have about who we are and what we think we want, and instead recognize ourselves as a part of the natural world, like the birds and the fish.

We each have two sides, our natural self and our creative self. Our natural self has no desires. It just follows the flow of our life deeply present, eats when hungry and sleeps when tired. The fish swim this way and that way with no desire to be something else or to live some other way. They just swim and eat and defecate the way fish do. On our creative side, we have the desire to do something that has not been done before, to create something, to get somewhere.

Our lives consist of both. And when we express our creative side, we see that we are always changing, always moving forward or solving some problem, and feeling excited. But when we are expressing our natural self, we aren't excited, nor are we concerned about novelty. We breathe. We drink water. We eat some food. And we go to the toilet when it's time to do these things. That's all.

When you see someone eating very fast because they need to go somewhere afterward, for an appointment, you know something's wrong. But if, even in the middle of a busy day when we're expressing our creative self, when we get hungry, we take the time to slow down and eat mindfully—that's natural. That's what's in front of us and what we need to do to take care of. Not to rush through it, so we can go back to our job and be excited again. We can feel satisfaction in the excitement of creativity, but we also need to find the deep satisfaction of experiencing ourselves in the natural world. I believe that fish and birds are always feeling satisfaction too.

Without the grounding of the natural world, the excitement of our creative selves will create problems for us. When we become addicted to excitement, even the excitement we feel using our creative skills, difficulties will follow. I live in Silicon Valley, and of course we encourage creativity. But at the same time, we encourage practice. This is how to live a balanced life even in the creative center of the high-tech world.

Our practice is the expression of our natural self, and through it, we can remember who we are and understand the meaning of the activities that take place in our lives. When we

I Had a Good Teacher 81

connect with who we are in the natural world, we won't be overwhelmed by our daily lives and we won't worry whether someone or something is good or bad. The point of our practice is not to be perfect. It is to understand our natural self, which means we are already perfect in the deepest sense. Zazen practice is an expression of this.

When you drink a cup of tea, you may find it hot or cold, bitter or sweet, but if someone asks you how it tastes, words cannot explain your actual true feeling. Only you can feel it. So, we just appreciate our awareness of the taste of the tea without trying to explain it. This is the awareness of our natural self.

Drinking tea has always been an important activity in Zen practice. We can know how to drink tea in the same way we know how to hear a bird or music. Just as we should know how to relieve ourselves in the restroom and we how to pass the milk at breakfast. And we should know how to create or discover something. But if our mind does not feel the natural world, its busy-ness and excitement can prevent us from dwelling deeply and enjoying these moments.

Bodhidharma, the figure who brought Zen from India to China, said, "Even if a Buddha should suddenly appear, there is no need for reverence. The natural mind is empty and contains no such forms. Those who hold on to such appearances, will go to hell." Bodhidharma may be a mythical figure and his words might not be literal, but this message is important: even if a Buddha should suddenly appear, there's no need for reverence or excitement. Our practice is to let go of excitement. Just pay attention to each thing. Then we will feel natural and know what to do. There will be no problem and no suffering.

20

THE ALIEN AND THE BANANA

IMAGINE A FLYING saucer landing and an alien steps out. He's a friendly guy, and he says "I've heard a lot about Earth. I hear it's a good place and you have some really wonderful things. I'm glad to be here." Then he adds, "I've also heard about your fruits, and I'd love to try one. I'm most interested in your bananas. But what's a banana?"

How would you describe a banana to someone who doesn't know anything about them? Perhaps you'd say, "They're yellow. And when they're not fully ripe, they're solid and firm." A good start. "And, by the way, they're slender and smooth." Very good. Those are characteristics of a banana's appearance.

When we describe bananas, or anything, we might talk about what it looks like. But the *nature* of a banana is not its peel. That's its protection, and it's smooth and firm. But the life-giving nature of a banana is on the inside. We can't see it at first look. So, we might say the true nature of a banana is in its softness, which is beneath the surface.

The explorations of our practice are like that. We want to see ourselves (and all living things) beneath appearances. Like a banana, we too are soft and flexible and our true strength is not on the outside, not what we display to the world. Our true strength is in our lifegiving qualities, like the fruit *inside* the banana peel.

Our practice is to understand and acknowledge our fundamental self without being misled by our protective skin. When we're able to practice vulnerability, flexibility, and openness, we can express our generous self. Softness and flexibility give life to our activities and relationships. That softness gives life to life. But when we hold on to appearances, it's because we fear our softness. We're afraid to give of ourselves, to peel off our outer skin, because doing so seems unsafe.

And when, to protect our small self, we have this fear, we develop a hardness to life. Then we believe that we are our skin, our appearance, and this trick of the ego is probably our greatest delusion. Because of it, we misunderstand ourselves. The peel of the banana is designed to protect the inside. But with a feeling of safety and confidence, we see that there is no need to protect our true self. *Our true self cannot be harmed.* It's the ego that needs protection.

Appearances can protect, but they're vulnerable. When you peel a banana, the peel cannot stand up by itself. The firmness of the fruit is in the soft inner part, not in the peel. Firmness on the outside has its purpose, but don't mistake it for your true self.

We shouldn't be misled by tough guys or tough women. Buddha was firm and strong, but he wasn't a tough guy. Dongshan, Dogen, and Suzuki Roshi were firm, but they were also soft-hearted and lifegiving. They stood up because of their softness. Our true self can never fall down.

When Dogen was in China, he asked his teacher, Rujing, "What is emancipation from body and mind?" Rujing replied, "Emancipation from body and mind is zazen."[27] His answer was very important for us. It means making an effort is to dedicate our whole body and mind to each activity. And it means to let go of body and mind, which means to see beyond appearances. It's a point we should study with our whole life.

Dogen wrote a fascicle titled "Dragon Song": "One day, Touzi, Great Master Ciji of Shu Region was asked by a monk, 'Is there a dragon singing in a withered tree?' Touzi replied, "I say there is a lion roaring in a skull.'"

Then Dogen added:

> Non-believers say that an old withered tree is just an old withered tree and ashes are only ashes. There is a great difference between the opinions of non-believers and those of the Buddhas and patriarchs. Non-believers discuss the concept of a withered tree, but they do not know what it really is. Much less do they understand the roar of a dragon. Non-believers think that a withered tree is a dead tree and will not have foliage next spring.[28]

Dogen can be a little tricky. If we try to analyze what he wrote, we might ask the meaning of "a lion roaring in a skull"? We know that's impossible, that it can't happen. How do we understand the world according to Dogen with our thinking mind? We can't, so we have to try another way.

Rujing replied to Dogen that emancipation *is* zazen. When we sit in zazen, we are never alone, even when we're sitting on our cushion by ourself in the zendo or at home. If you think you're sitting alone, you're really saying, "I'm just an old withered tree." *To sit alone is to roar like a dragon.* To say that a withered tree has no life is a misunderstanding. Even a dried-out skull can roar like a dragon. So, when you're in zazen, the whole universe is practicing zazen. When we forget this point, our sitting becomes difficult. Doubts and resistances arise.

My advice is whether you feel alone or at one with the universe, just keep sitting, and little by little you'll come to appreciate that you're never alone. And you can say to yourself, everything is sitting and I will join them. When you come to the zendo and see that no one else is here, that's just its appearance. The zendo, even when it's empty, is roaring like a dragon. It may look like a withered tree, but pretty soon, there's fruit. If you see yourself as just yourself, it may be difficult to sit. When we see things in a limited way, when we see life only as appearances with a protective cover, we'll have a hard time coming to zazen. We'll resist giving of ourselves, and we'll lose a big opportunity. We have to see ourself as not-self to be emancipated from body and mind. When that happens, we are no longer a banana still wrapped in its shiny yellow peel. We are the fruit, the marrow of practice.

BEAUTY BEYOND BEAUTY

In Zen temples throughout the world, monks, nuns, and lay people chant the Heart Sutra regularly. At Kannon Do, we recite it every Saturday morning, and in Japan, they chant it three times a day. The Heart Sutra, one of the most important scriptures of Mahayana Buddhism. It was created around 200 CE, and some scholars call it the purest distillation of wisdom.

The Heart Sutra describes the emptiness of self and all things. One line says: "Form is emptiness. Emptiness is form." When you first hear that line, it may be confusing. It's difficult for the mind to hold opposing ideas at the same time, and you may wonder where you are and what they're talking about. We have form—things, people, and objects—and emptiness. What is this emptiness?

In the last year of his life, Suzuki Roshi gave a talk explaining the purpose of practice. He said that zazen, "just sitting," *actualizes emptiness* in our lives so we can see beyond our ordinary ideas about the world.[29] "Form is emptiness, and emptiness is form" helps us connect with a world beyond the limited perspective of our intellect. It's not exactly a separate place or dimension, but a different way of seeing things—based on not just the appearance of solidity of things, but their emptiness.

Emptiness points beyond our everyday reality. When we start to appreciate this so-called other world, we can let go of ideas we hold that were programmed in us by our culture, parents, schools, and friends. Suzuki Roshi explains that when we practice zazen, we get a glimpse of the emptiness of the world, and after that we're more able to accept things as they are without bias or wishing they were different. But when we can't appreciate the empty nature of things, we become self-oriented and our understanding narrows. Our feeling about ourselves and others becomes limited if we see the world only as form. Understanding emptiness, we develop a reverence for all things. Without it, we run the risk of inattention, separation, and a lack of intimacy. We crave connection with each other, and it can slip away if we don't see things clearly.

We have many conveniences, things that we have and can do that were unbelievable fifty years ago. But even though we have all this at our fingertips, the degree of anxiety in society is increasing, and the sense of satisfaction seems to be decreasing, partly because we are more and more dependent on our conveniences. Here's an example. When you enter a dark room, if you want light you turn on a switch. If there's a motion detector, it turns on the light for you. A hundred and fifty years ago, you had to light a candle or a lantern, remove the glass chimney, strike a match, turn up the wick, carefully put the chimney back on, and then carefully pick up the lantern. Having to perform all these steps focused our attention on creating light. We were creating light and were paying attention to it. Now we're very casual about bringing the miracle of light into our room, and if we aren't mindful of how we turn on the switch, it becomes a kind of a throwaway activity. It doesn't even register that we're doing it. This is the danger of conveniences. We run the risk of not being engaged.

Layman Pang, a Buddhist adept in ancient China, wrote a poem that ended with the words: "My spiritual practice is carrying water and chopping wood." These activities are the work of survival. If you wanted to heat your home or cook your food, you had to chop wood to make a fire. And if you wanted water to cook, drink or bathe, you had to get it from a well and carry it in a bucket.

I don't think many people complained that they had to chop wood. They had to do it; it was part of their life. Today we hardly think about where our water comes from and how convenient it is to turn on a tap. We don't think much about how our house is heated either; the thermostat turns the heat on automatically. When people chopped wood or hauled water, I suspect they often felt satisfaction in doing it.

We cannot go back to a world without conveniences. Nobody is suggesting that. But if we want to regain intimacy with basic activities, with the way we relate to the world and bring light, heat, and water into it, we need to regain that intimacy through zazen practice.

Our practice is so vital these days because we are losing touch with the things that make us feel very engaged. For example, when you turn on a light switch, pay attention to your hand touching the switch and the movement of the switch. And when you turn on the stove, pay attention to how you turn it on and how the flame or electrical coil starts up. When we pay attention to these ordinary activities, we get a glimpse of the world of emptiness. This is why this practice is so vital.

If you're at home reading or writing on your computer and your friend or partner comes to you and says, "Hey, let's have a coffee," you might say, "I can't, I'm too busy." You think you want them to leave you alone, but more likely than not, it means your mind is not ready.

Try saying, "What a great idea," knowing you can go back to your reading or writing later. This is an opportunity to be intimate. We call it "ready mind," a mind in balance, a mind of no attachment. When we are always ready for intimacy, for connection, this is the world of emptiness, not trying to attain anything, just being present to the energy flow of each moment.

When you sit in meditation, don't hope to gain anything, not even stress relief. Seeking always includes the idea of a self, and when the idea of a self is involved, our practice cannot come to balance. The striving of the self throws us off balance, and we can't return to emptiness. When we practice, when we sit in zazen, we try to let go of seeking, wanting, and desiring. We just sit, and return to emptiness.

When we hear, "Form is emptiness, emptiness is form," we can say to ourselves, hmmm, let me try to understand that. In a short time, we'll discover that we can't get to the truth of emptiness by thinking. To empty everything, we have to go back to where no idea of anything arises. Suzuki Roshi gave this example of a glimpse of emptiness. He spoke about how much he liked to create miniature Zen gardens with small stones, small plants, and small trees. He seemed to be endlessly creating a small garden around his cabin at Tassajara Zen Mountain Monastery. Then one day he walked to Tassajara Creek to collect more stones and when he saw the rocks in the water in their natural place, he thought, I can't do this anymore.

Sometime later he invited a friend, a master gardener, to visit him at Tassajara to help him with his garden. They walked to the creek together to pick up some stones, and his friend said, "I don't want to work on the rock garden. I would rather clean Tassajara Creek by taking out the papers and cigarette butts. Let's take care of Tassajara Creek and not worry about the garden." Suzuki Roshi described this, saying, "A beautiful miniature Japanese garden copies nature, but in nature, there is beauty beyond beauty."[30]

One of the problems we have as human beings is that we analyze our experiences. We are so into studying and explaining everything we do, see, and feel, but we cannot measure our experiences or our feelings, our intimacy and our love. Trying to measure them, we're taking a picture for the thinking mind to hold on to. But a picture of our experience is not our experience. Our experience has no dimensions. It cannot be measured, and it cannot be confined.

Our practice is to see things with a wider mind and to see them as empty. Our sincere zazen practice and the attitude that motivates us will actualize emptiness in our life. It's not that life is empty, but the true nature of our life cannot be measured. With practice we can see things as they are, fundamentally and originally before we add something and "spoil" the reality.

When Suzuki Roshi and his gardener friend went to Tassajara Creek to look for stones, they decided to leave them there and pick up the trash instead. Our practice allows us to see things as they are. When you sit, don't let your mind be disturbed by the noises that come up. Let it rest. Don't let your thinking mind tell you who you are. There isn't another dimension. You just need to experience reality without measuring. This is our practice. And it's the door to emptiness.

PART TWO

PERSONAL STORIES

22

THE MAGICAL WORLD OF FISH

The Museum of Natural History, across from New York's Central Park, was an easy three-block walk from my childhood grammar school. That school is long gone, but the museum—which opened in 1869—remains an international destination. When I was in school, our classes had annual outings there and it was the second most enjoyable day of the year for us. Guides showed us replicas of prehistoric and modern birds, elephants, lions, tigers, giraffes, wart hogs, hippos, rhinos, gemsbok, oryx, wildebeest, dinosaurs, and my favorite, the dik-dik—animals we didn't see on the streets of New York. My classmates and I felt as though we had been transported to another time and place, and were living in the wild.

The most enjoyable days, though, were class trips to the New York Aquarium on the boardwalk at Coney Island, an hour's subway ride from our school. The oldest marine museum in the U.S., it too is still open. My friends and I would stand wide-eyed, looking at hundreds of bright-colored species of diverse marine life swimming in the tanks. In contrast to the exhibits at the Museum of Natural History, here we *entered* the fishes' magical world. Even we raucous kids could feel a sense of peace and calm in their flowing movements. Every visit there was fresh and new.

On one aquatic outing, as I watched fishes of myriad shapes and sizes swim up to the glass that separated us from them, then quickly dart away, I realized that despite their seemingly carefree existence, they were captives in that tank. I had a strong sense of these marvelous beings longing for freedom, a return to their natural home in the boundless oceans.

We humans share the same basic urge to be natural and authentic, unconfined by manmade boundaries. Yet to feel safe and supported, we follow society's customs, limiting our lives to cherished traditions, and paying the price of the very freedoms that would bring us to wholeness.

As infants, unable to take care of ourselves, we don't have the option of selecting what's on the dinner menu, or even feeding ourselves. We rely on adults to spoon-feed us. Somebody older plans and serves the menu. At that age, it's no problem: we accept the arrangement. Hunger relieved, we feel satisfied by whatever we've been fed.

Maturing into youth, a second type of hunger emerges, the desire to make our own decisions and act independently. We want to go beyond being "spoon-fed" and learn for ourselves how to live, no longer dependent on others. Then, adulthood brings a third hunger—to be free of ignorance and confusion. This is the hunger for truth, wisdom, and knowing who we are—the foundation of spiritual seeking.

Yet through all the stages, we're at risk of being "spoon-fed" by teachers, authorities, books, media, and gurus. Our parents, family, school, government, and the whole spectrum of our culture influence and shape our minds before we gather our experiences and develop our own world view and intuition. These influences can keep us from finding ourselves for our whole life. If we are too easily satisfied by what we are told early in life, we'll have little interest in making discoveries. Instead, we follow the script of other people's ideas.

For our lives to be authentic, we have to reflect and make our own discoveries, not clinging to spoon-fed beliefs. If we don't turn away from the script to find ourselves and our voice, we're no different from the wooden man and the stone woman of the "Song of the Jewel Mirror Samadhi,"[31] who were not free to sing and dance. Zazen practice helps us become aware of the fixed images of the past and come alive in the continuously flowing ocean of our lives.

23

BEING NICE

ONE WARM LATE summer evening, in a popular Upper East Side Manhattan steak house in the early 1940s, I was in youthful high spirits. My father had brought me along to dinner with his friends and business associates, jovial, confident, and good-humored men. I could see that they enjoyed being with my dad and I was getting a lot of attention.

Shortly after cocktails arrived, one of my father's friends asked me, "So, young man, what are you going to be when you grow up?" I answered, "Nice." He explained, "I mean, don't you want to be a doctor or a lawyer or an engineer or an architect or a businessman like your father?" I sat in silence, gazing at the bubbles rising in my ginger ale, too young to imagine what it might be like to work in any of the professions he suggested. But I did know what "nice" felt like. I was eight or nine at the time.

New York is known for its crowds and busyness. People bump into each other and get in each other's way. Subways and buses don't have orderly queues; instead, there is pushing and shoving to get on even before exiting passengers can get off. The resulting bottlenecks last less than a few seconds with no flow in either direction. Yet in that brief time, the results can be friction, anger, and tension.

New Yorkers are also polite and considerate. I often heard "Pardon me," "Good morning," and "Please go ahead." When politeness was expressed, I felt the world ebb and flow with a natural rhythm, without conflict, relaxed.

Nice has a universal meaning that extends beyond everyday courtesies. Social conventions are needed to sustain a functional community, but they are limited in reach, touching only the surface of relationships. Our practice asks us to take *nice* to the next level, to make it inclusive beyond casual greetings and expand our motive from courtesy to empathy and taking care.

Buddhism orients our lives toward the elimination of worldly suffering, and we start with paying attention to the ways we relate with one another, focusing on who and what are in front of us. Relieving suffering, in ways large and small, is continuous. It's not an activity we turn on like a light switch only when needed, forgetting about it when suffering isn't apparent. Relieving suffering is an attitude that continues without a break.

In Zen practice, the emphasis on taking care of ordinary activities is illustrated by the following story:

> Two monks are on pilgrimage, traveling from temple to temple, visiting and studying with well-known teachers to expand their practice and understanding. Walking beside a creek, they approach a well-known monastery. A vegetable leaf appears, floating downstream. The monks pause in dismay, and prepare to turn around and retrace their steps. Suddenly another monk comes out of a side door, running toward the creek with a long pole. He stops at the edge of the water, reaching out to retrieve the truant leaf. The

two monks smile and quickly resume their journey to the temple.[32]

The foundation of spiritual practice is a commitment to creating a world permeated by *nice*, what Suzuki Roshi meant when he referred to our "inmost desire." The world of *nice* is a world of no separation, a world of caring and flowing. We have a long tradition of creating such an environment.

More than twenty years ago, a member of Kannon Do wrote the following poem:

> Those who flow as life flows
> Need no other force
> They feel neither wear nor tear.
> May I flow like
> Silk thread on a sharp needle
> Through soft cloth.[33]

24

THE BODHISATTVA WAY

WHEN I STARTED college in the early 1950s, I was confident that my education would provide the foundation for what I'd need to live the American dream. At the time, prospects for engineers were on the rise, promising interesting, well-paying careers and comfortable lifestyles. I felt no need to think about studying anything else. But a college experience exposes and stimulates the young mind to wider possibilities, and liberal arts classes opened my imagination to a world beyond logical, scientific thinking. This experience from more than seventy years ago remains vivid today.

In September, with football in the air, Literature 101 began with the study of Greek drama. It was like nothing I had ever come across. Until then, I was interested only in the objective, modern worlds of technology and sports. Lit. 101 introduced me to subjective realms—myth, poetry, and literature—subtle worlds, undefined, beyond the ordinary.

The semester started with the study of "Prometheus Bound," said to have been written by the playwright Aeschylus sometime in the fifth century BCE, based on the myth of the half-god-half-human Prometheus. In the legend, Prometheus looks down from heaven, sees the suffering of humankind, and gives it the gift of fire. This act infuriates Zeus, and the most powerful of the gods punishes Prometheus in a cruel and painful way. He's chained eternally to a rock in space where an eagle returns each day to eat his replenished liver. Now, the myth of Prometheus is far more complex than this short synopsis, but suffice it to say, I was relieved to learn that Prometheus is eventually freed.

Being half-god, Prometheus knows what is in store for him. Yet he makes the most profound personal sacrifice out of his sense of compassion for the suffering of the race of human beings. The legend dramatically illustrates—even proclaims—the caring nature of the hero whose sensibility is not confined to myths, or to a few uniquely gifted individuals on the planet. Without exception, everyone has this inherent heroic potential. It is our true nature.

Extraordinary heroic actions of ordinary people are the greatest of gifts: risking one's life to save the lives of strangers. We see this every day when firefighters ignore their own safety to enter burning buildings. In 1955, Rosa Parks refused to move to the back of the bus. On January 6, 2020, in Washington, DC, a lone Capitol police officer diverted members of the mob from entering the Senate chamber, possibly saving lives. In the early 2020s during the pandemic, ICU nurses worked incredibly long hours at great risk to their own health and well-being. Their passion for the work and sense of caring is compelling. In a letter to the editor, a nurse in Virginia summed up the heroic quality: "If you don't know a nurse, you don't know somebody who has compassion the size of the universe—so we're going to be there and we're going to make sure that patient doesn't die alone."

Yet there are as well many less dramatic types of heroes among us—unnoticed, quietly living modest lives. In some religions, they are known as saints. In Buddhism, they are the bodhisattvas who work to relieve spiritual confusion and suffering by teaching the Dharma, engaging others with kindness, and giving of themselves in the moment. In Mahayana mythology, bodhisattvas forsake their own entry to Nirvana so they can remain in the troubled world and guide all beings to enlightenment.

Compassion can be expressed wherever help is needed, not only in life-threatening circumstances or heroic deeds. The only prerequisite is selflessness—the motivation to live without too much concern for personal well-being. It is beyond measure, manifesting from understanding life's true value-added: taking care of each other and the world we live in.

The indifferent, cruel, and all-powerful Zeus is the personification of the unpredictable, often harsh life on earth. The humanity of Prometheus, his inherently caring nature, leads to the relief of suffering. It is the foundation of our spiritual practice.

25

HIJACKING AWARENESS

I STARTED WORKING for IBM in its new product development laboratory in San Jose, California in 1958. In those days of barely emerging technology, IBM dominated the business machines environment. Companies of every size, in every industry, were heavily invested in those mid-twentieth-century, electromechanical devices, the first to automate handling and processing of digital information. Punched cards were everywhere—in desk drawers, file cabinets, purses, wallets, coat pockets, and glove compartments.

On my first project, I joined a small team of engineers and machinists developing a process for transporting and reading a new prototype design for a punch card containing three times as much information as the original card. If we were successful, the so-called "advanced" card would significantly improve the capacity of IBM card-handling machines.

I found the work exciting and satisfying—designing, building, and assembling physical components, running tests with prototypes of the new card, analyzing data, and refining the design. Executives flew in from New York for demonstrations.

One morning, following two years of progress and

optimism, my boss assembled our team in his office. He announced that the project was cancelled, explaining that IBM was initiating a new approach to its business, one that did not involve punched cards. The senior engineer asked about the new strategy. The boss replied: "Something called software."

Fast forward from the early 1960s through the creation of the World Wide Web, the internet, personal computers, tablets, servers, and smart phones. Information from sources everywhere became instantly and continuously available. Today we have ads, websites, social media, opinion pieces, commentaries, blogs, YouTube and TikTok videos, and 24/7 news. The hardware-oriented "business machines" era ended half a century ago; now we are in the "information age," often referred to as the "attention economy." As a result, our mental radar is always "on," our awareness subject to an overwhelming abundance of news, opinion, and entertainment.

We increasingly live online, giving much of our attention to the cyber world. Competition for our attention is pervasive—media, advertisers, and politicians want our money, our votes, and our loyalty. Brands, organizations, and belief systems promise a better life. Along with conspiracy theories that are not entirely truthful, they try to create compelling narratives to highjack our attention. The constant pressure makes us vulnerable and makes us victims. It's a major source of stress in today's world.

But hijacking of the mind—a form of mental theft, an intrusion into our awareness—did not start with modern software. It has always been with us. More than 2,000 years ago, Buddhism recognized how the inherently aware mind can be compromised, not by ads, social media, or societal forces, but by our own thoughts, desires, and distractions. That is how we victimize ourselves.

Chapter two of The Dhammapada emphasizes the necessity of being unconditionally aware, remaining in our natural awakened state, undistracted:

> Wakefulness is the way to life.
>> The fool sleeps
>> As if he were already dead,
>> But the master is awake
>> And he lives forever.
>> How happy he is!
>> For he sees that wakefulness is life
>> How happy he is,
>> Following the path of the awakened.[34]

To be wakeful is to be in total awareness full-time, as though continually bathed in moonlight, while the fool, lulled to sleep by distractions, does not even notice the moon. In *Zen Mind, Beginner's Mind,* Suzuki Roshi writes, "I discovered that it is necessary, absolutely necessary, to believe in nothing. That is, we have to believe in something which has no form and no color—something which exists before all forms and colors appear."[35]

What exists before all forms, colors, and things of the world is Awareness, Buddha-mind. Awareness is sacred in Buddhism, rather than external deities. Zazen practice keeps Awareness accessible by enabling us to recognize and let go of distractions. Every discriminating thought or act of uncaring hijacks awareness.

26

LIKING MYSELF

Soon after I graduated from college, I entered the U.S. Army as a second lieutenant, thanks to the ROTC, the Reserve Officers' Training Corps that prepares college students for military service leadership. The Korean war had ended three years earlier, but the draft of able-bodied young men was still in force. ROTC allowed me to delay military service until I graduated.

I was stationed at Aberdeen Proving Ground (APG) in Maryland, a one-hour drive from Baltimore and two hours from DC. I instructed new recruits and career officers in radar electronics.

After work on Fridays, officers would gather for happy hour to socialize and develop personal relationships, unrestricted by rank. One of my friends—a major—was a psychologist in the APG (Ambulatory Patient Group) hospital, a man I respected for his humor, intelligence, and amiable ways. On a warm evening in June, he abruptly changed the course of our conversation with a startling comment, "Why don't you like yourself?"

Totally shocked, I became defensive, insisting that of course I liked myself. But my carefully crafted sense of myself was abruptly shattered. For several days I struggled to push aside my friend's words, not accepting his well-meaning, non-judgmental perception. Yet over the course of the following week, I became less defensive, slowly admitting he was right. I was not entirely comfortable with how I was living my life.

It was a painful recognition, urging me to pay closer attention to the ways I conducted myself in everyday relationships, to become increasingly aware of my feelings, words, perceptions, and gestures. Bit by bit, I started to recognize habits and tendencies that arose without warning from some hidden place, impulses that undermined attentive awareness. Over time, they became less intrusive, increasing my sense of stability and ease.

After Aberdeen, in 1958 I migrated to San Jose, starting a career that had good prospects. I married a lovely, smart, caring young woman with a quiet sense of humor. We started a family and had good friends with whom we enjoyed exciting times.

Yet despite the good life, I retained an uneasy feeling that it was somehow artificial, lacking what truly mattered. It was as if a window to a wider reality was darkened by heavy shutters, preventing recognition of a dimension beyond the confines of the ordinary.

In the mid-1960s, I came across Zen. Its world view struck a chord immediately, just as when a haiku poem touches us with sudden immediacy, a sense of clarity, and we feel: yes, exactly right!

Zen teachings proclaim a spiritual practice without religious dogma, with emphasis instead on each of us discovering wisdom through our own awareness and efforts. The practice points toward living a life of authenticity, avoiding role playing and posturing. Making adjustments in family and work life, I become immersed in the practice.

Zen discourages pursuit of success, teaching that reputation—including acquired knowledge and fame—is merely a flattering poster of our self in the everyday relative world but does not represent who we are inherently. What is more important, the carefully constructed and guarded image is not a valid criterion for "liking" our self. Life's confusion and suffering are created by not appreciating who we are in a universal, spiritual sense, by not recognizing our intimate, inseparable relationship with all things. Here we find the basis for "not liking" our self, and it's what Zen practice encourages us to uncover.

My friend, the major, was a modern-day version of the traditional no-nonsense Zen master, helping his student to see his true nature. Ten years after our conversation, I found Dogen's message in the *Genjo Koan*: "To study the Buddha Way is to study the self. To study the self is to forget the self. To forget the self is to be actualized by myriad things. When actualized by myriad things, your body and mind as well as the bodies and minds of others drop away."[36]

Intellectually and emotionally, studying the individual self of our day-to-day world is the starting point for discovering the undifferentiated, impersonal spiritual self. Non-thinking zazen quietly sets the mind at ease, casting off ideas of a small "self" of feelings, desires, and ambition, leaving no "self" to dislike.

When we receive a friendly nudge about our self from an acquaintance, teacher, or especially from our own sense of discomfort, we should not turn away from it. Rather, we should consider that it has merit—facing it directly, exploring it honestly without hesitation. It is the first step on our journey of spiritual discovery.

27

SIMPLICITY AND EASE

Suzuki Roshi described how we get lost when we're caught up in excitement and the overwhelming busyness of daily life. In 1969, a year before his book *Zen Mind, Beginner's Mind* was published, I experienced this truth face to face.

In the fall of that year, still new to Zen practice, I attended a ceremony at the San Francisco Zen Center, followed by an informal lunch where we all sat at long tables in the dining room. I was across from Suzuki Roshi and I felt a rush of anticipation. I have so many questions, I thought. Here's a chance to ask one.

Not wanting to seem anxious or intrusive, I waited for eye contact to occur by chance. But Suzuki Roshi never looked up; his eyes remained on his food. Remaining silent, I observed how attentively he picked up his bowl, how he embraced the simple meal with care.

My eagerness to ask questions went into remission; my compulsion to speak evaporated. I kept my awareness on the mindful way he handled his utensils and bowls, and by contrast, how I handled mine. The quiet meal ended with the sound of clappers, two wooden sticks hit together as in Zen monasteries, and a short chant. We bowed, our eyes met across the table, and we greeted each other, spoke for a few moments, and parted. I no longer felt the need to ask a question. From that time, I just wanted to live with such simplicity and ease, not caught up in eagerness for stimulation and attention.

We come to practice because we want to live truthfully, without guile, to know the fundamental truth at the heart of our lives, beyond the layers of complexity. We want to see life with clarity, in its most simple terms, so that there is no confusion, no need to speculate a meaning. Yet our overactive, analytical mind can easily lose the quality of simplicity.

Continuous, consistent practice enables us to see our impulses and desires, to recognize our ego in action, how it protects the image of a made-up self. Zazen practice trains the mind to suspend the frantic currents of mental activity, to see our life with humility, to quiet our insistence on emotional arousal.

Establishing Zen practice in the United States faces a number of challenges, including how our modern way of life continually creates multiple energies and how it uses and is used by them. In today's world, we are attracted to excitement, inspired by high energy, demanded of us as expressions of creativity and leadership in industry, sports, entertainment, and politics, necessary to achieve personal and social goals. So our mission at our Zen centers is faced with a challenge: how can our quiet, contemplative, selfless practice penetrate the walls of the never-at-rest, ambitious, goal-oriented world we live in?

As we explore this vital question, little by little we gain understanding. It is not a short-term project; there is no guarantee of success any time soon, but the way the world is going, the effort is necessary.

Buddhists and Zen practitioners understand how we are led astray by the pursuit of goals and success, how we compromise with the truth. And we understand that trying to outwit life is futile. We practice so that we can feel alive by seeing and living the truth, not by ego-fueled concerns derived from personal ambition.

In the Flower Sermon Sutra, disciples assemble to listen to a talk by the Buddha. Remaining silent, he holds up a flower. The monks do not understand his gesture, except Mahakashyapa, who smiles, and so becomes the Buddha's successor.[37] Suzuki Roshi's way inspires us by quiet confidence and simplicity, rather than high energies. Enlightenment—the truth—is simple, close at hand.

28

I HAD A GOOD TEACHER

I**T'S STILL DIFFICULT** for me to believe that Suzuki Roshi accepted me so readily and completely as one of his disciples. I know now that it stemmed from his open and compassionate nature and his full acceptance of everyone. However, like other Los Altos students, I didn't see him very often and felt hesitant in approaching him or taking any of his time: He "belonged to" San Francisco Zen Center, I thought, and we were lucky enough to see him once in a while.

When I did go to him to speak about becoming ordained, I went with a hesitant, cautious feeling. We exchanged greetings and became silent. He asked me why I wanted to be ordained. I gave him a reason that was not very profound, in fact it was rather ordinary. Without a word, he stood up, went into the other room, and came back with Okusan (Mrs. Suzuki) and a tape measure. Immediately they began measuring me for robes. I let them turn me, tape me, hold my arms out, and listened to them discuss the finer details of tailoring for the next hour. I left in a kind of daze, unsure when my ordination would take place, only that it would take a few months for the robes to come from Japan.

Suzuki Roshi was always at the center of things. He did

not need words to understand a situation. He could take it in instantly, hardly observing it. He had a great kindness and never hesitated to go someplace or do something when requested. And he had that wisdom to say the words or do the thing necessary at the moment. As an example, I remember how he handled a particularly anxious moment at my ordination in January 1971. The ceremony had begun, and we were crowded together in the Los Altos Zendo, when my mother arrived. She was anxious about the strange, unorthodox step her son was taking, and all eyes were on her as she entered the zendo late. I'll never forget Roshi's look, glancing at her as she entered and took the seat for her near the platform. Very gently he reached over, put his hand on her shoulder, and said, "You came at the right time."

So, I became one of his disciples. But I didn't visit San Francisco Zen Center very often, again for fear of disturbing him or taking his valuable time. I did make it a point to see him at least once every three months. I didn't want to run to him with problems, but I did want to be with him occasionally, so I told him whatever was of greatest concern to me at the time.

I wasn't really sure of all the formalities and once I asked him if we were having *dokusan*, the formal teacher-student interview/encounter in Zen. He said no, that it was just a student visiting and having tea with his teacher. In every way, he just let things take their own natural course without pushing.

He provided encouragement when he had the opportunity, as he always invited me to come back, but never said "should" or set a date—it was up to me. I realize now that I could have visited him twice a week or more, if I had wanted to.

Suzuki Roshi had a great sense of humor. He was always smiling. He laughed easily at even the smallest whimsy. Whether at a formal party prepared in his honor, or eating the simplest meal at Zen Center, he gave the impression of enjoying himself tremendously.

He was also a little mischievous. Once when we were at Tassajara, my wife Mary, who is a bonsai enthusiast, found an oak tree and dug it up. She eagerly showed it to Roshi, who said, "Oh, thank you very much," and took it away, leaving Mary open-mouthed.

Dainin Katagiri Roshi[38] once asked Mary and me if our zendo was ready for its own teacher. We thought about it, discussed it with others, and later told him we were ready. We asked him what to do next, and he said to see Suzuki Roshi for advice on who to invite. I spoke to Suzuki Roshi about Katagiri Roshi's suggestion, and he proposed that we invite Kobun Chino Sensei[39] to return to the U.S. to be resident teacher of the Los Altos group.

Months later, after Chino Sensei arrived, it dawned on me that the whole thing had been planned by Suzuki Roshi with the help of Katagiri Roshi. Catching two birds with one stone (getting Kobun and making us independent), he worked it so that we did the soul-searching and decision making, and took the necessary steps.

Suzuki Roshi died on December 4, 1971, a little less than a year after my ordination. I sometimes regret not being able to be with him physically anymore. But then I think of how lucky I have been just to have known him, for however brief a time, and to have been accepted by him so completely.

His memory fills me completely. I try to do things with his spirit in mind, not because he is "watching," but because he trusts me. He trusted everybody, even before he met them.

29

THE ZEN PRACTICE OF STEVE JOBS

WHEN STEVE JOBS passed away on October 5, 2011, the media paid tribute to his genius, accomplishments, and contributions to societies around the world. Included in the stories were items about his spiritual seeking, in particular his pilgrimage to India—when he was nineteen—and his Zen marriage ceremony in Yosemite National Park. Less well-known is the *depth* of Steve's spiritual orientation, the time he spent exploring and practicing Zen Buddhism in the mid-1970s and how that period influenced the design of Apple's products that are in the hands of what sometimes seems like everyone on the planet.

Although I've told parts of this story throughout the book, I'd like to share it one more time, with a little more detail. In 1964, Zen master Shunryu Suzuki, who had arrived in San Francisco from Japan five years earlier, began a small meditation group on the peninsula, south of San Francisco, in what is now Silicon Valley. I joined this group in 1966. Suzuki gave weekly talks following sitting meditation, which were recorded on a huge five-inch reel-to-reel Wollensak tape recorder, the state of the art in recording technology in those days. They were transcribed, edited, and published as *Zen Mind, Beginner's Mind*, still one of the bestselling and clearest introductions to Zen practice.

As the group grew larger, Suzuki asked me to invite Kobun Chino to come from Japan to serve as resident teacher. Kobun was a caring, intuitive, warm individual, and people delighted in his presence. With him as spiritual leader, more people from the peninsula joined the group. One of them was Steve Jobs, recently returned from India. Steve admired Kobun, and they developed a close student-teacher relationship. They had long, private talks, sometimes at midnight while walking the streets of Los Altos, the home of the Zen group as well as Steve's hometown.

I met Steve during this time. He was twenty, a college dropout, and a sincere seeker. I was in my forties, working for IBM, and raising a family. By then, I had been ordained a Zen priest, had a regular meditation practice and a number of responsibilities with the group, and thus had dual careers—Zen and work in the everyday world.

Even though Steve was pretty much a hippie at the time and I was clearly part of the establishment, he came to see me often with fundamental life questions. "What is work? What is its value? Does it have meaning?" he asked during our first meeting. I saw him as idealistic, even a bit naive, but I also recognized him as a deep soul who wanted to understand the nature of life and his place in the world. At another meeting, he asked, "You work for a large corporation, have a family, and are very involved in Zen. How does it all go together?"

In those days, western Zen students were mostly products of the '60s, trying to establish alternative lifestyles, skeptical of middle-class values. Many of my younger co-practitioners were dubious of my dual life, that I could be a Zen priest without dropping out. This never seemed to be an issue for Steve. I felt no sense of skepticism from him. He seemed eager to learn from my experience as part of his exploration of spirituality in work. He thought a lot about how it could be part of a competitive business environment. I didn't have satisfactory answers for him at the time and suggested we pursue the question. But in less than a year, Steve left the group.

On a Saturday afternoon in 1976, Steve showed up at my house unexpectedly. He had a large folder of schematic drawings and asked if I'd review them. "What are they?" I asked. He replied, "I can't tell you. It's something I'm working on." I said, "There's a lot here. These would take hours to review, and I haven't been in engineering for ten years."

I didn't think I could help, and I apologized. He picked up the drawings and left, saying, "That's okay. Sorry to trouble you." I was surprised to see him with circuit diagrams, unaware of his collaboration with Steve Wozniak, an electronic wizard who Steve Jobs met while he was still in high school.

A few days later, I realized that he hadn't come to see me for technical input on the diagrams. He wanted to know if I felt the design was *spiritual*. He didn't say so directly and I have no way of confirming this intuition, but knowing Steve's passions from our past discussions, I feel sure that's what it was. He had found a place for himself in the emerging high-tech world but didn't want to close off his spiritual dimension. I'm certain he wanted some kind of Zen aesthetic in whatever he designed and was asking if I could see it in the circuitry.

By 1998, Apple had become hugely successful. That year, I started a Meditation at Work program to present meditation practice—its relevance to issues of life and work—to Bay Area organizations. My steadiest client was Apple. A number of times over the years, I was able to meet with Steve after class for lunch in the cafeteria. Steve was pleased I was bringing Meditation at Work to Apple. I asked if he had continued his

Zen practice—"Just occasionally," he admitted. But he continued to be influenced by its principles.

We talked about dedicating a room for meditation at Apple's Cupertino site. Steve jumped at the idea. He took me on a tour of the campus to look at possible rooms for the class. He asked the vice president of human resources to help me create a program. We developed a plan to have Apple engineers participate on a voluntary basis, one work group at a time. But busy schedules intervened and rooms were scarce. Classes were often postponed or delayed because of impromptu meetings. Although Steve was supportive, the plan never got off the ground. Today, priority for classes and meditation rooms in the workplace is much higher.

Despite what the media might allege and what Soto Zen headquarters in Tokyo would like the world to believe, Steve never became a fully devoted Zen student. In fact, he continued to maintain his interest in the teachings of Swami Paramahansa Yogananda, whose book *Autobiography of a Yogi* was given to everyone who attended his memorial service at Stanford.

However, he continued to explore the expression of Zen practice in the workplace. He resolved it in his unique way, through the design and function of Apple products. To many, especially during Steve's lifetime, Apple was itself a kind of religion, its adherents deeply devoted to its product line. Apple's computers, phones, and other products reflect simplicity, imagination, and creativity, along with uncompromising quality. He always had the end-user in mind, not simply as a customer, but as a person whose life could be improved. The products, born of Steve's vison of creating a Zen aesthetic in them, broke barriers of what was thought to be possible. He provided his own answers to his questions of spirituality and work.

30

NO DRAMA

THE YEAR 2020 marked the fiftieth anniversary of the publication of *Zen Mind, Beginners Mind*. This inspiring collection of Suzuki Roshi's plain-speaking Dharma talks—presented at Haiku Zendo in the 1960s—has introduced Zen practice and its relationship to daily life to millions of ordinary people in the United States and around the world.

Thanks to this book, Suzuki Roshi became famous for his spoken words. Yet he had a less public dimension that eloquently expressed his wisdom in the immediacy of the present moment. The following story is one example of the quieter side of our founder.

In December 1966, energized by Suzuki Roshi's vision of Zen in America, San Francisco Zen Center purchased the Tassajara Hot Springs resort in the Los Padres National Forest, which extends from Big Sur to the Salinas Valley in Monterey County, California. In July the following year, it opened as the first Zen monastery outside of Asia. For the next several months, interest and excitement grew in the U.S. among the increasing number of scholars and writers who had been exploring Buddhism since the mid-twentieth century.

In August 1968, after two years of Zen practice and three months prior to moving to Haiku Zendo as resident caretakers, my family and I scheduled a three-day visit to Tassajara, open to guests during summers. Our weekend coincided with a significant event: the formal initiation of Suzuki Roshi's monastery in America.

When we arrived midday Friday, an entourage of eight Japanese Zen teachers had already been at Tassajara for several days. Saturday morning was the highlight of the weekend: Suzuki Roshi and three other well-known roshis were introduced to an assembly of more than a hundred scholars and students, all crowded into the zendo, the converted bar and lounge of the early 1900s resort.

Yasutani Roshi was eighty-three at the time. Since 1962, he had been traveling between Japan and the U.S., conducting *sesshin*, seven-day silent meditation retreats, never staying in one place. He was a dynamic presence, emphasizing the use of koans, using the *kyosaku* (so-called "awakening stick"), yelling at students, and criticizing the Soto Zen school as being soft-hearted.

Soen Nakagawa Roshi, a Rinzai priest, helped found the Dai Bosatsu monastery in upstate New York. Described as enigmatic, he was dramatic in voice and gestures.

Eido Tai Shimano, a Dharma heir of Nakagawa Roshi, founded the Zen Studies Society in New York City and the Dai Bosatsu monastery. Each of the three visiting roshis gave rather lengthy talks, followed by questions from the audience.

When the questions ceased, a silence came over the zendo.

I stood up and asked the final question: "What is the best way to spread Zen in America?" The three roshis huddled, along with Maezumi Roshi from the Los Angeles Zen Center, who was translating. He announced that each roshi would answer the question in turn.

Yasutani Roshi forcefully emphasized, "Get enlightenment!" and "You must die!"

Nakagawa Roshi was vocal and demonstrative. He emphasized building zendos.

Shimano Roshi was also dynamic and dramatic, walking back and forth across the stage. His message was: "Do sesshin!"

When it came his turn to speak, Suzuki Roshi stood up, said "I have nothing to say," and walked out the side door of the zendo.

The three guest roshis provided the kind of answers we expect in everyday affairs, rational responses to questions we ask of individuals who have more knowledge of a subject than we do. Suzuki Roshi literally turned his back on all that.

Informative, commonsense answers do not always serve us well in our efforts to find wisdom and authenticity. Zen is famous for turning away from the thought processes of a rational mind, instead responding to the moment unencumbered by memory, unexamined experiences, or an entrenched belief. Teachers abruptly reoriented a question or dialog, providing enigmatic responses without explanations. Their purpose was to keep their disciples off-guard, avoiding the smugness of a well-defined answer.

Consider another, ancient example of this. We read how Bodhidharma treated emperor Wu in China, who asked him, "What is the highest truth?"

Bodhidharma responded, "Vast emptiness, no holiness." Centuries later, a monk asked Zhaozhou: "Who is Buddha?" Zhaozhou replied: "Who are you?"[40]

Suzuki Roshi was mindful of how he answered questions. As he says in *Zen Mind, Beginner's Mind*: "A mind full of preconceived ideas, subjective intentions, or habits is not open to things as they are."[41]

As he walked off the platform and out of the Tassajara zendo that day in 1968, he expressed Beginner's Mind with very few words. At Kannon Do we continue the practice begun at Haiku Zendo over fifty years ago. We are all Suzuki Roshi's successors in the twenty-first century.

AIM FOR THE HEART

DURING THE 1960S, the Haiku Zendo, later to become Kannon Do, was a small meditation hall in what had been a garage of a private home in Los Altos. It was named the "Haiku" Zendo, because when Marion Derby's garage was converted into a zendo there was space for seventeen meditators, and a haiku poem has seventeen syllables.

As I've mentioned, Suzuki Roshi came from Japan to serve as minister for a Japanese Soto Zen congregation, Sokoji, in San Francisco's Japantown. Over time, young Americans, including many hippies, found him and his wisdom there, and began to join the meditation periods at Sokoji. In 1962, the "new Buddhist" sangha incorporated as the San Francisco Zen Center, continuing to meet at the Japantown temple.

In 1967, Zen Center acquired 160 acres in the Los Padres National Forest and opened Tassajara Zen Mountain Center as the first Zen monastery outside of Asia. And in 1969, Zen Center bought its own building in the Hayes Valley neighborhood of San Francisco, not far from the Haight Ashbury district. Suzuki Roshi resigned from Sokoji and moved into the Zen Center's new home, a beautiful, large building designed by the legendary Julia Morgan.

In those early days of Zen in America and the Bay Area, Suzuki Roshi would travel once each week from San Francisco to Los Altos, with a Zen Center student as his driver. Following zazen, his Wednesday evening lectures included a question-and-answer dialog with these Santa Clara Valley Zen students.

One of those students was Allan, a smart, energetic, gregarious young man, always ready to laugh. He was in his mid-twenties attending medical school at Stanford. His girlfriend, Beth, was also a graduate student at Stanford. A great future was anticipated.

One Wednesday evening, Allan had a question for Suzuki Roshi:

> Allan: Roshi, I am very afraid a lot of the time. I am afraid now. Can you help me?
>
> Suzuki-roshi: Afraid of something of which you cannot figure out, you mean?
>
> Allan: I think I'm afraid of being hurt, and then lost.
>
> Suzuki-roshi: Lost? No, it is not possible to be lost. You are here, and there is no need to be afraid. Maybe you are afraid because you are changing and because everything is always changing. But if you are always changing, why don't you try to change for the better? As long as you make that kind of effort, there will be no need to be afraid of anything. Even a little bit of change for the better will work.

Roshi saw Allan's plea for help not as a problem to be solved analytically or emotionally, but as a spiritual dilemma. So, he did not ask: What is it that you are afraid of? as might a psychologist or psychiatrist. Instead, he encouraged Allan to embrace his own true nature, to accept that he—along with everyone and everything—is constantly changing. And he subtly nudged Allan toward a creative approach to his fear and a more positive view of himself.

Few of us will admit to being fearful; usually we hide our vulnerability. But Allan felt safe asking his question in front of others, feeling supported by fellow Sangha members and his teacher. Suzuki Roshi demonstrated that support by offering an optimistic world view for Allan to consider: it is not possible to be lost.

A year later, Allan died suddenly of a heart attack. The Haiku Zendo community was shocked. He had no known history of illness.

In our humanity, we try to create a path for our life that will provide opportunity, satisfaction, and peace of mind. Yet despite our best efforts, inevitably and without warning, life presents us with tragedy, confusion, or fear. Not knowing what will come along, our best response to impermanence and disruptive change is to continue our practice in the midst of uncertainty, to reflect on the truth of our lives, to nurture our community, and to live each day with optimism.

Not everyone is fortunate to have the support of a community like ours. We continually meet with people who are feeling emotional pain about what is happening around the world. They feel fearful and lost; we should stay sensitive to that truth. To everyone we meet in our everyday lives, we can speak to the mind when necessary, but we should always remember to aim for the heart.

32

QUESTIONS AND RESPONSES

Editor's Note: At the end of many of his Dharma Talks, Les Kaye invites questions. Here are some students' questions, with his responses.

How do you practice feeling compassion for someone who has done something extremely wrong? And specifically, how do you avoid feeling the emotion of pity for them as opposed to compassion?

When we feel that someone has done something harmful or has a habit of doing that, before we condemn, before we get angry, before we want revenge, we have to acknowledge that that person is suffering. I don't believe human beings do harmful things if they don't feel they've been harmed or that they are being harmed now. Only when we suffer are we at risk of doing harmful things.

So, when we experience someone like that, we have to know they're suffering. Starting from there, from that compassionate mind, we can assess what might be the best way to respond. There's no formula, no one thing. The response to someone who is creating harm is different in each case, depending on where their suffering is coming from. So, we try to understand the other person before we start to think about how we should treat their suffering. And this desire to understand is a form of compassion.

*

Some relationships are unhealthy. They can be codependency or in the realm of addiction or mental illness. We may have the concept of tough love, where you have to do something unpleasant or maybe discontinue contact with the other person. How does the idea of tough love relate to what you just said?

Generally, we get tough when we see or know that there is stubbornness and that displaying generosity, kindness, or compassion won't be sufficient because their mind is stuck. So, we try to help with that, to loosen their toughness, and the *tough* part of tough love tries to help the other person see how they are limiting themselves. Doing so requires going beyond expressing some feelings and taking some action. During the many recent tragedies of mass shootings, certain public figures say, our thoughts and prayers go out to all these people. They just send out these words. Tough love means finding some way to do something to get the problem resolved.

*

My question is about loving yourself. It seems to me that to love and accept yourself, you have to, in some part, be attached to the way that you are and the things that you like to do and even the stuff that you have that makes you you. How can we fully love and accept ourselves while remaining true to our practice, so that attachment does not get in the way.

It's hard to feel good about yourself, to love yourself, if we have to have some particular thing. "If I don't have it, I won't like myself." That's kind of foolish. I can like myself, I can love myself, whether I have this or not.

There's so much pressure these days—you must have the latest. It's a burden. We have to learn to be wary of that kind of pressure that comes at us from all over. I sometimes ask myself, if for some reason I couldn't come here anymore and be with you, would I be okay? Am I attached to all of this? Sometimes in life we have to give up things that have made us feel comfortable and feel good. We lose them or they're taken away or they move away. If we have a strong practice, we can continue feeling confident and strong and good about ourselves, even if we lose what seems so vital to us.

*

When Emperor Wu asked Bodhidharma, "What is the highest truth?" Bodhidharma replied, "Vast emptiness, no holiness." If he really said that, why do we revere images of the Buddha and the patriarchs and the ancestors?

We can have more than one attitude toward the images of the Buddhas, or the idea of the Buddhas. One is to simply pay our respects and express our gratitude for what they did, for the effort they made. It's just an expression of gratitude. When that's what it is, when that is the meaning behind what we do, when we bow or keep a good thought toward Buddha or Suzuki Roshi, we are showing some understanding about effort and character, and what people can do for each other.

But if we get carried away emotionally with Buddha and believe there are some kind of magical powers, this misunderstands what they did. Reverence in the form of gratitude is pretty healthy. Reverence in the form of supplication, giving up ourselves for something we think is greater is a misunderstanding. When Buddha appears, we can just say thank you and not get excited. That is what Bodhidharma said and it's the kind of attitude we try to develop.

*

You've said many times that there is no suffering in the natural world. If by "natural world" you mean plants and the environment, I kind of agree. But the natural world includes animals. If a mother deer raises a baby and a wolf comes and takes it away, I'm not sure there's no suffering. If a crow in the road dies by accident or whatever, the whole extended family gathers and they don't move for fifteen or twenty minutes. I see that when I'm driving, and I feel there is suffering in the natural world.

There are difficulties and disappointments and loss and grief every day. But the crows who come to mourn the dead crow, they don't say, "Why did this happen to me?" They don't suffer that way. They just say, "Oh, that's the way the world goes. The wolf will catch the deer. That's the natural world. We can't stop that. But the mother of the deer doesn't say, "Why did this happen to me?" There's a loss and there's sadness, but it is not suffering. There is a difference. This is a kind of fine point that, as we practice more, we appreciate more.

*

In your talk you made a distinction between the natural and the creative things we do. I don't understand what you mean by that. Birds do amazingly creative things. They build beautiful nests and find creative ways to avoid creatures that are coming to eat them. Are you saying we shouldn't think that washing the dishes, cleaning the bathroom, or doing things that are "natural" are not important, and that only creativity is important? Are you suggesting not to give more value to creative or work-related activities, but to treat everything we do as equally important?

Yes. We normally think that when we're creative, somebody will like it and we'll get approval or they'll buy it or something like that. Birds don't have these kinds of ideas.

We can become attached to the notion that creativity is only present if someone approves or buys it. If we judge our life that way, we'll miss the creative things we do that have nothing to do with approval or buying. We want to appreciate the moments when we've been creative and no one noticed. That gives us a deep feeling of satisfaction. When you clean your house, if you take care of everything and don't take shortcuts, that's creative. When you finish, you can say, "I did it." You're making a good point.

*

Can you explain the difference between feeling numb, just not responding to things, and being centered and more in a natural state?

Sometimes we feel numb, and sometimes we feel energetic. If we can be aware of ourself at all times, we will recognize these two different states and notice or try to notice what's happening. Where is this numbness coming from? What's going on with me? Or where is this excitement coming from? What's going on?

When we come back to ourself and know how we're doing, we don't get carried away by either the excitement or the numbness. And when we can see why we feel this way or that way, we can see if there's anything we need to do.

Maybe we don't need to do anything. Maybe I'm numb right now, and that's all right. But numbness can be a form of suffering. When we notice that, we can try to determine how to come back to ourself. It's about *noticing* how we are, how we have gone off-center with either numbness or excitement. How do we come back to the balance, to the "natural feeling"? The more we practice, the more we are familiar with the balance. And the more we recognize what it feels like to be balanced, the more we practice.

*

The quote you read by Dogen about believers sounded sectarian to me: "The withered tree spoken of by those outside the way and that spoken of by buddha ancestors are far apart. Those outside the way talk about a withered tree, but they don't authentically know it; how can they hear the dragon singing? They think that a withered tree is a dead tree which does not grow leaves in spring." What do you think he meant by "those outside the way"?

Dogen is referring to those people who are stuck in habitual ways of doing things and don't have the flexibility to see things in new ways. To the believer, a belief may feel like a way of seeing. But if there is stubbornness in that belief, then it is not seeing. It is just believing without reflection, without open mind, or as Suzuki Roshi would say, without Beginner's Mind. In one of his talks, Suzuki Roshi said, and I have found also, that it is absolutely necessary to believe in nothing.

*

Can you explain what you meant by "The banana peel is to protect what's inside. But there is no need to protect our true self."

It's not a matter of inside or outside. If we see our true nature, our true self, as if it were the inside of some fruit, then we fear that it will get hurt. But our true self, our larger self, is beyond inside and outside. And when we go beyond limits of inside and outside, nothing can be hurt. There is no such thing as hurt. It's a matter of appreciating who we are inherently. Inherently, we are neither inside nor outside.

*

You said, "We shouldn't be misled by stories of tough guys. Buddha was firm, but he was not a tough guy." My question is, we tend to value firmness over toughness, but the popularity of tough guys is not going away, as we see in Hollywood. What makes them stick around? Why are we not getting rid of tough guys?

We can never get rid of anything. But when we accept things as they are, tough guys are no longer tough guys and we don't need to be frightened by them. If we accept everyone for who they are, there are no more tough guys. But if we are at war with them and try to get rid of them, it's impossible.

*

How do you stay connected with the people you loved who have died, like your teacher Suzuki Roshi?

The people who were most significant to me when I was "seeking," those who made an impression, are indelibly etched in my

134   **Les Kaye**

mind. I don't need to make an effort; they are always there and they pop up at certain moments without me even trying.

You raise a good point, that if we're fortunate, we have people in our life who touch us by expressing the qualities we admire. And when we meet them and they touch us in a deep place, we never forget them. We are never separated from them. Once we make that connection, it takes no effort at all to keep them in our mind and heart.

*

You said, "When the flower is alive, it is the flower; and when the flower dies, it is the flower." My question is, When I am alive, am I myself? When I am dead, am I myself?

You are yourself, and at the same time you are much more than yourself. This is what we learn when we pay careful attention to our life, to how we are in the world, and to how we are with others. I am me, but at the same time I'm more than me. I'm not separate from others. This is the paradox of our practice— that there is no separation between you and everything else, but of course we feel separate.

And this is the question we all ponder: The teachings tell us that there is no separation. Why, then, do I always feel separate? We pursue this enigma with our practice. There's no easy answer, sorry.

*

Suzuki Roshi said, "We are perfect as we are, but we can use a little improvement."[42] As students we put emphasis on the improvement side, so I appreciate your talk on the first part of the sentence, "We are perfect as we are." How do we re-center our practice on the perfection side of the equation. Is focusing on the larger view, including all of our life and death, the way?

When we are quite serious about our practice, and by that I mean when we want our practice to help us be as complete and authentic as possible, our effort will express our perfection. When we're casual about the practice, we won't make as much of an effort to express our perfection. Because we want to be complete and authentic, and not compromised, we keep our attention on everything we do so we don't trip up and betray our perfection. We notice the little imperfect things we do from time to time, which are the places we can stand some improvement.

I think Suzuki Roshi was encouraging us to pay attention, to try to improve ourselves continually, to go beyond the things of our mind that distract us from who we are. When he says, you can use some improvement, he is saying you must continuously come back to yourself and not get lost in your distractions. And when you make the effort to be as attentive, mindful, and heart-centered in each moment, you express your perfection. But it is difficult to do that, so we have to try to improve.

It's a clever and humorous saying, and it's also quite serious. If Suzuki Roshi had said, "You're perfect just as you are," I don't think it would be as helpful. But he goes on to say, "You have to make an effort continuously." He is challenging, admonishing, and encouraging us to express our true self. The humor he brought to his teaching was part of his great gift. Even in this moment, I feel I have one more thing to say in response to your question and I want to be sure I get it right. So, I'm paying attention to what's arising in my mind and how my words are forming. This is how I try to improve myself.

*

You said that life and death are the same. They don't seem the same to me; death is a loss. Can you say more about this?

Yes, of course. There will be a loss and grief when someone we care for passes away. This is not a negative thing; it's just how we feel. Some day when the grief passes and we don't feel as sad, we will remember that person and say: "She was quite wonderful. She was perfect." We're humans. We have emotions and it's painful when we lose someone like that. So in the moment when someone passes away, it does not feel perfect at all, but that's the way it has to be. We appear and later we disappear. Our role is to take one step at a time, and along the way, our feelings will come up. How do we keep our equanimity in the face of loss or in the face of pain? We can discuss that more another time.

*

I understand the difference between "striving" vs "making an effort." Is there something like too much of an effort? We want to live effortlessly, you know.

Our body and mind recognize when we can't make any more of an effort. If I have a flat tire and want to change it, and if I try to take the lug nuts off the wheel and they're too tight, after making a big effort, at some point I need to recognize, "That's enough. I can't do it."

We need to try, and then we need to recognize our limits, doing what we can without creating suffering or anxiety by trying to do what we cannot. It takes being honest with ourselves, honest about our capabilities and limits, and not try to overdo it. It's okay to stop when something is beyond what we can do. I think our body and mind know when we have reached our limit.

*

Does striving include an expectation, an attachment, and an action, while making an effort is pure and detached?

Two weeks ago, you said how good washing the dishes makes you feel. Just taking care of things. If someone were to have asked you, "What is your goal?" you might have replied that it isn't a relevant question. You just made the effort to wash those dishes to help everybody, but you weren't striving to accomplish something. You just did it, without attachment, because it gave you joy. If we can do everything with that attitude, there wouldn't be any confusion.

That's how we hope to be in all our actions and relationships—to do them smoothly and naturally without striving, simply because it is joyful to do it. It's easy with the dishes, because they don't have much of a personality. They don't say, "You didn't dry me enough." It gets trickier when we're with another person.

I came across this saying in the Dhammapada: "Let us leave happily, totally detached, freeing ourselves from the anxiety of losing all that is ours."

*

Do you think this practice attracts people who have a keen sense for perfection, not only in the sense of wholeness but also in the sense of making an effort and not feeling relaxed with oneself or having confidence in oneself? I'm like that. You've seen many students; do you think there is a tendency, maybe because of the strict forms of Zen practice, for people of this kind to come to practice? I've met people who are attentive but more relaxed who might not have the drive to practice sitting meditation, who might need another way to learn about the Buddha's teachings.

I think people are attracted to Buddhist practice because it promises completeness, to fill up what feels incomplete, and to feel in tune with life. We come to the practice because we don't feel complete, because we're out of touch with something we feel we want to be in touch with.

No matter how successful we are in life, how intelligent we might be, or energetic or creative, we're always at risk of feeling incomplete and out-of-tune. We need to take a break from our everyday life and return to the fundamental practice of "home-leaving"—taking a break, sitting on the cushion, going into nature, going to a monastery—putting aside the part of our life that pushes us to strive and gain so we can see our entire being. Then we can go back to the striving part of our life with a greater sense of wholeness and a better understanding of what kind of effort we want to make.

BRING YOUR CARING NATURE TO LIFE

IF YOU ARE lucky, sometime in your life you will have an experience that will reveal who and what you are. It will hint at the possible direction of your life. It could be a thought, a feeling, an activity, or a word, much like the future Sixth Patriarch who, it is said, had an awakening upon hearing the Diamond Sutra. He dropped everything and immediately joined the Zen community of the Fifth Patriarch. However, if your experience is to influence or impact your life, your luck needs to include your recognition and acknowledgment of the experience, so that it remains as a guide and not evaporate like a cloud.

The revelation is not always immediate; it usually doesn't grab our attention right away and move us to action or deeper reflection, as in the story of the Sixth Patriarch. It may take years to realize the insight and what it opens for us.

But once the experience is embraced, how should we respond to the new knowledge? We could note it as interesting, but then judge it as not being significant enough to do anything about. Or, we could reflect on what it means, or should mean: Is it strong enough to consider altering the course of our life? How heavily does it influence our attitude and world view?

I had such an experience as a young boy. It was in 1942. I was eight years old, living in a busy New York City neighborhood. The United States had recently entered World War II. There was no TV news to show us what was happening, but movie theaters showed newsreels of the warfront. Images of the death and destruction in Europe were frightening and confusing for everybody. I was just a kid but I had an adult thought of, what is the reason for the cruelty and killing?

Also, in daily life, I saw how people kept rubbing each other the wrong way in the crowded, speedy, noisy, dirty streets of midtown Manhattan: so much pushing, shoving, threatening each other to get some kind of small advantage, like being first in line at the grocery store. Then I had another thought: Why are people so mean to each other? These questions did not go away.

There were churches and synagogues in every direction within a few blocks of my street. All the religions preached kindness, peace, charity, and community. And all were based on a relationship with a powerful, external being that could influence lives. When I thought about all the suffering in the world, that part of the religious vision made no sense. I thought, Why would a benevolent, loving god allow that? So, in my preteen years, I learned not to trust any religious belief system.

Twenty years later, living and working in the paradise of Santa Clara Valley, married to the woman of my dreams, I serendipitously came across Buddhism. It spoke of kindness, peace, generosity, discipline, and community. What struck me immediately was the absence of dependency on an external deity. Buddhism's message seemed to be, there is wisdom and love here, but you have to do the work.

The legend of Buddha tells us that Buddhism and Zen

practice started because all human beings are touched by suffering. The Buddha was moved by his recognition of what he saw happening in human life. He felt something personal; he cared and he wanted to take care. He did not seek for easy answers to humanity's problems and suffering outside of the lives and relationships of humanity itself. He emphasized practice, awareness, integrity, and development of moral character. He encouraged his followers to make a serious effort to understand the meaning of their lives.

Meditation by itself is not enough to activate kindness, peace, generosity, understanding, and forgiveness. What is needed is an attitude of caring and a willingness to do the work of practice. We can't just sit here and expect wisdom to appear without doing the work.

If you travel to Japan, Vietnam, or South Korea, if you ask lay adherents or Zen monks, "How did you come to Buddhism and to practice," most will answer, "I was born into it." Unlike in western countries, there is very little diversity of spirit among the Buddhist churches and centers in Asia. But we in the U.S., UK, Europe, and Latin America are in "discovery mode," trying to understand and establish this new practice on new ground. It is creative, exciting work, and with it there is a big responsibility.

In addition to the role of luck in leading us to explore spiritual practice, there is always a causal condition. Our wake-up experience is not random; it does not come from nowhere; it can only grow out of awareness and sensitivity to the realities of the world. It happens because we have kept our spiritual radar turned on.

You come to this practice because you feel something, and this feeling has moved you. You have come to learn about this practice because you care, because you are not indifferent to the difficulties and sufferings of life. I encourage you to take it seriously—the feeling, and the passion you feel for it. Be patient as you acquire wisdom and skillful means through the practice. Make your best effort, pay attention, learn as you go, and don't let this opportunity be blown away by the breezes of doubt. Do not be tentative or hesitant in your practice, which only leads to sleepwalking. Go beyond saying, "Well, maybe I will," to "Yes!" and bring your caring nature to life.

We are lucky to have Zen centers, including Kannon Do, to practice together in a supportive community. Let's continue the work we have started, caring about the authenticity of our own lives while taking care of each other and everyone and everything we meet.

ZEN ANCESTORS CITED IN THIS BOOK

Pinyin (Chinese)	Wade-Giles (Chinese)	Romaji (Japanese)	Chinese	Dates
Baizhang Niepan	Pai-chang Nieh-p'an	Hyakujō Nehan	百丈涅槃	d. 828
Dayi Daoxin	Ta-i Tao-hsin	Dai Dōshin	鑑智僧璨	580–651
Dazu Huike	Ta-tsu Hui-k'o	Taiso Eka	大祖慧可	487–593
Deshan Xuanjian	Te-shan Hsüan-chien	Tokusan Senkan	德山宣鑒	780–865
Dongshan Liangjie	Tung-shan Liang-chieh	Tōzan Ryōkai	洞山良价	807–869
Guishan Lingyou	Keui-shan Ling-yu	Isan Reiyū	潙山靈祐	771–853
Longtan Chongxin	Lunt-t'an Ch'ung-hsin	Ryōtan Sōshin	龍潭崇信	9th century

Pinyin (Chinese)	Wade-Giles (Chinese)	Romaji (Japanese)	Chinese	Dates
Mazu Daoyi	Ma-tsu Tao-i	Baso Dōitsu	江西馬祖道	709–788
Nanquan Puyuan	Nan-ch'üan P'u-yüan	Nansen Fugan	南泉普願	749–835
Su Dong Po	Sū Dōng Pō	Sotoba	蘇東坡	1037–1101
Tiantong Rujing	T'ien-t'ung Ju-ching	Tendō Nyojō	天童如浄	1163–1228
Xiangyan Zhixian	Hsiang-yen Chih-hsien	Kyōgen Chikan	香嚴智閑	d. 898
Yaoshan Weiyan	Yao-shan Wei-yen	Yakusan Igen	藥山惟儼	745–828
Yunju Daoying	Yün-chü Tao-ying	Ungo Dōyō	雲居道膺	830–902
Yunmen Wenyan	Yün-men Wên-yen	Ummon Bun'en	雲門文偃	864–949
Zhaozhou Congshen	Chao-chou Ts'ung-shên	Jōshū Jūshin	趙州從諗	778–897

NOTES

[1] Editor's Note: Shunryu Suzuki Roshi used the Japanese transliterations (Romaji) for the names of most of the Chinese Zen masters he spoke about, and Les Kaye did that as well. Throughout *I Had a Good Teacher*, we use modern Chinese (Pinyin) romanizations of these teachers' names. At the end of the book is a chart of these ancestors' names in Pinyin, Wade-Giles (older Chinese orthography), Romaji, and Chinese characters.

[2] For more about koans, see Thomas Cleary and J.C. Cleary, *The Blue Cliff Record* (Shambhala Publications, 2005), especially the book's introduction. This is Case 70, pages 473-476.

[3] The story is adapted from "The Taste of Banzo's Sword," Case 91 in Paul Reps, ed., *Zen Flesh Zen Bones: A Collection of Zen and Pre-Zen Writings* (Charles E. Tuttle, 1957), 98.

[4] From "Genjōkoan," a fascicle by Eihei Dogen, founder of the Soto School of Zen Buddhism in Japan. See, e.g., Kazuaki Tanahashi, ed., *Moon in a Dewdrop: Writings of Zen Master Dōgen* (North Point Press, 1985), 69. In this book, Les Kaye relies on several translations of Dogen's writings.

[5] There are many translations of the *Heart Sutra*. Here is the character-by-character translation that was used as San Francisco Zen Center when Les Kay studied there. https://www.cuke.com/Cucumber%20Project/other/heart-sutra/heart-sutra-card-2.html

[6] Shunryu Suzuki, *Zen Mind, Beginner's Mind* (Shambhala/Weatherhill, 1970), 53-55.

[7] Adapted from The Lotus Sutra, Chapter 12. See, e.g., Burton Watson, trans., *The Lotus Sutra* (Columbia University Press, 1993), 183.

[8] In Zen practice, it's customary to follow the tradition transmitted by one's teacher. Some, for example, teach us to meditate while facing the wall, while others have their students sit facing the center of the room.

[9] Kazuaki Tanahashi, ed. and trans., "Valley Sounds, Mountain Colors" in *Enlightenment Unfolds: The Essential Teachings of Zen Master Dogen*, (Shambhala Publications, 1999), 64-65. Co-translated with Katherine Thanas.

[10] This story is told in Tanahashi, *Enlightenment Unfolds,* xix, and in Takashi James Kodera, *Dogen's Formative Years in China: An Historical Study and Annotated Translation of the Hokyoki* (Shambhala: 1980). 37. Quotes are adapted from "Instructions for the Tenzo," in Tanahashi, *Moon in a Dewdrop*, 58-60. Co-translated with Arnold Kotler.

[11] Suzuki, *Zen Mind, Beginner's Mind*, 62.

[12] Su Dong Po's poem and the commentary by Dogen are from "Valley Sounds, Mountain Colors," in Tanahashi, *Enlightenment Unfolds*, 59-60. Co-translated with Katherine Thanas.

[13] This story is adapted from *Shumon Kattoshu,* Case 26, "Xiangyan's Sound of a Bamboo," in Thomas Yuho Kirchner, trans., *Entangling Vines: A Classic Collection of Zen Koans* (Wisdom Publications, 2013).

[14] "Ordinary Mind Is the Way," Case 19 of the Gateless Gate (Gateless Barrier), is quoted in *The Dewdrop*, October 28, 2019. Trans by Katsuki Sekida. https://thedewdrop.org/2019/10/28/ordinary-mind-is-the-way/

[15] Quoted by "r/zen" in https://www.reddit.com/r/zen/comments/2w7v9i/guishan_baizhang_shows_guishan_the_ember/?rdt=54473

[16] From Alan Watts, *The Way of Zen* (Vintage Press, rev. 1999), 132.

[17] A version of this story appears in Urs App, trans. and ed., *Zen Master Yunmen: His Life and Essential Sayings* (Shambhala, 2018), 205.

[18] Quoted in Norman Fischer, *Training in Compassion: Zen Teachings on the Practice of Lojong* (Shambhala, 2013), 42.

[19] *Dogen Zenji's Shōbōgenzō (The Eye and Treasury of the True Law),*

trans. by Kōsen Nishiyama and John Stevens (Daihokkaikaku, 1983). 21.

[20] "A Question and Answer Session with Suzuki Roshi," July 8, 1969. https://cuke.com/pdf-2013/srl/v25-2-quetion-answer-session.pdf

[21] "Continuous Practice," in Dogen, *Treasury of the True Dharma Eye*, Vol. 1, trans. by Kazuaki Tanahashi. Co-transated with Sojun Mel Weitsman and Tensho David Schneider (Shambhala, 2010), 364-365.

[22] Nishiyama and Stevens, *Shōbōgenzō*, 98.

[23] Adapted from "Nishiyama and Stevens, *Shōbōgenzō*, 20.

[24] Guo Jun, *Essential Chan Buddhism: The Character and Spirit of Chinese Zen* (Monkfish Book Publishing, 2013), 19.

[25] Suzuki, *Zen Mind, Beginner's Mind*, 57.

[26] Adapted from Nishiyama and Stevens, trans., *Shōbōgenzō*, 20.

[27] This story is told in Kodera, *Dogen's Formative Years in China*. See Josho Pat Phelan's commentary on this encounter, https://www.chzc. org/sesshin-talk-1-on-fukanzazengi-by-josho-pat-phelan.htm

[28] Nishiyama and Stevens, *Shōbōgenzō*, 198.

[29] Shunryu Suzuki, "Letters from Emptiness: How to Understand the idea of Emptiness" (Dharma talk, March 8, 1970, San Francisco Zen Center). This lecture was the basis of the chapter of the same name in Shunryu Suzuki, *Not Always So: Practicing the True Spirit of Zen*, ed. by Edward Espe Brown (HarperCollins, 2002), 35.

[30] From Suzuki, *Not Always So*, 37.

[31] Zen poem from the time of the Chinese Song dynasty (ninth century). See https://thedewdrop.org/2019/05/08/dongshans-hokyo-zanmai-song-of-the-jewel-mirror-samadhi/

[32] Told in Les Kaye and Teresa Bouza, *A Sense of Something Greater: Zen and the Search for Balance in Silcon Valley* (Parallax Press, 2018), 173.

[33] Nancy Smee, untitled poem, from an early edition of the *Kannon Do Newsletter.*

[34] Verse 2, "Wakefulness," from *Dhammapada: The Sayings of the Buddha*, trans. Thomas Byron (Shambhala Pocket Classics, 1993).

[35] Suzuki, *Zen Mind, Beginner's Mind*, 116.

[36] Anonymous translation of "Genjokoan." https://genjokoan.com.

[37] This story is told in many places. See, e.g., Heinrich Dumoulin, *Zen Buddhism: A History* (World Wisdom, 2005), 9.

[38] Dainin Katagiri (1928-1990) came from Japan to the Soto Zen Temple in Los Angeles, then joined Suzuki Roshi at the San Francisco Zen Center to assist with the teaching. After Suzuki Roshi died in 1971, Katagiri Roshi founded the Minnesota Zen Meditation Center in the Twin Cities.

[39] Kobun Chino (1938-2002) was ordained a Soto Zen priest in Japan at the age of twelve. In 1966, at Suzuki Roshi's suggestion, the Haiku Zendo invited him to come from Japan to be their resident teacher. He accepted and arrived in San Francisco in June 1967. After he visited the Haiku Zendo, Suzuki Roshi asked him to spend the summer assisting him at Tassajara. Kobun Chino ended up staying at Tassajara for two years, making a short visits to Los Altos when he could. After that, he guided the practice at the Haiku Zendo from 1970 to 1978, and then at Hokoji, near Taos, New Mexico.

[40] This is the first case of the Blue Cliff Record. See Cleary and Cleary, *Blue Cliff Record*, 1-9.

[41] Suzuki, *Zen Mind, Beginner's Mind*, 88.

[42] Suzuki, *Zen Mind, Beginner's Mind*, 92.

ABOUT THE AUTHOR

Les Kaye has been integrally involved in developing Zen practice in the U.S. for over fifty years. He started work for IBM in San Jose, California, in 1958 and for more than thirty years held positions in engineering, sales, and management. In the mid-1960s, he became interested in Zen and started Zen practice in 1966 with a small group in the garage of a private home. In 1970, he took a leave of absence from work to attend a three-month practice period at Tassajara Zen Monastery in California. The following year he was ordained a Zen priest by Shunryu Suzuki Roshi. He took an additional leave of absence in 1973 to attend a second practice period at Tassajara, this time as head monk. In 1974, Les received Dharma Transmission, authority to teach, from Hoitsu Suzuki, son and successor to Shunryu Suzuki. In 1985, he was appointed teacher at Kannon Do Zen Center in Mountain View, where he is now Abbot Emeritus. Les is the author of three other books on Zen. He and his wife, Mary, have two adult children and live in Los Altos, California.

Kannon Do Zen Meditation Center brings the spiritual practice of Soto Zen Buddhism to the San Francisco Peninsula and the South Bay, including Mountain View, Sunnyvale, Palo Alto, San Jose, and surrounding communities, emphasizing its relevance in the modern world. Its purpose is twofold: to provide the opportunity for individuals to explore the spiritual dimension of life and to bring balance to busy lives faced with constant distractions, work and family pressures, and demanding deadlines. Kannon Do offers a vibrant community for practicing Zen meditation, exploring Buddhist teachings, and discovering ways that Zen can be expressed in the activities of daily life.

Kannon Do is a non-residential center, voluntarily maintained and supported by its members. There are no membership requirements to participate in its activities. The center welcomes all individuals interested in exploring Zen practice, regardless of race, ethnicity, or sexual orientation. Visit https://kannondo.org

OTHER ZEN BOOKS FROM MONKFISH

Zen Mind Jewish Mind: Koan, Midrash, and The Living Word
Rami Shapiro

"Not into Zen? Not a Jew? Not a problem. Anyone on any path will benefit enormously from this profoundly illuminating book." —**Philip Goldberg**, author of *American Veda*

With reference to Shunryu Suzuki Roshi's classic *Zen Mind, Beginner's Mind*, Rami Shapiro begins with beginner's mind as "empty, free of the habits of the expert, ready to accept, to doubt, and open to all the possibilities. It is the kind of mind which can see things as they are, which step by step and in a flash can realize the original nature of everything." Then, Rami ponders beginner's mind in the child of the Passover Haggadah "who knows not how to ask." The parents of this child are told to open (*patach*) the child to the art of questioning. *Zen Mind / Jewish Mind* rests on Shapiro's fifty-plus years of playing in the garden of Judaism, Zen, and advaita/nonduality.

Practicing Safe Zen: Navigating the Pitfalls on the Road to Liberation
Julie Seido Nelson

While the liberation that Zen offers is real, it must be engaged with carefully, explains this sensei. Her book is neither a memoir about a single case of abuse nor a bloodless academic study. Nelson reflects on the multiple dangers in Zen, from firsthand experience in Boston—where documented abuse recently took place—integrating her discussion at every step with core Zen teachings.

"*Practicing Safe Zen* imparts a lesson we all will have to learn if we want to truly mature in our spiritual practice." —**Barry Magid**, author of *Ending the Pursuit of Happiness*

Zen at the End of Religion: An Introduction for the Curious, The Skeptical, and the Spiritual But Not Religious
James Ishmael Ford

"Trappist monk Thomas Merton wrote, 'Zen is a way of insight.' Then he suggested what Zen is not: a system or method to be institutionalized, the way western society has domesticated religion. James Ford's insightful and honest introduction to this venerable tradition of meditation and inner transformation just might help us see what Merton meant—and why Zen can be a great blessing for our time, even for those who identify as spiritual but not religious." —**Carl McColman**, author of T*he New Big Book of Christian Mysticism*

Ford presents Zen as the ideal path for those who have left institutional religion behind.

AVAILABLE FROM BOOKSELLERS EVERYWHERE
MONKFISH BOOK PUBLISHING • RHINEBECK, NEW YORK

www.ingramcontent.com/pod-product-compliance
Lightning Source LLC
Jackson TN
JSHW082342190425
82662JS00001B/1